My Grief Jar

My Grief Jar

Still Growing After the Loss of My Daughter

A memoir by
Deborah Waffle

My Grief Jar: Still Growing After the Loss of My Daughter
Copyright © 2024 by Deborah Waffle

All rights reserved.

Cover Design by Shawn Jonas
Interior Layout by Rachel Newhouse for elfinpen designs

Author's Note

The names of physicians, teachers, and medical staff
have been changed.

For my daughter,
Kelsey Marie

Prologue

People lingered for days after the funeral. I appreciated their support, but all I really wanted was to be alone. When Marty left for work, the house was empty for the first time in twelve days.

I put Brody, my daughter's 18-month-old golden retriever, in his crate, and latched the door. I wasn't comfortable leaving him loose in the house, since he hadn't been here for long. It wasn't my belongings that concerned me. I wanted to keep him safe. He had napped in his crate at Kelsey's with the door open, so I thought he'd be more comfortable in there, even with the door closed. Especially when Max—my much older golden retriever—was snarling at him through a gate.

I got in my car and drove to Kelsey's house. The keys to unlock the mudroom door were still in my purse. Now, I used them before entering the kitchen, my heart pounding, my body rigid with fear.

What I needed most was to see the couch. Marty and I had bought the brown, velvety sofa for Kelsey because it had recliners on each end. Sitting in a reclined position had seemed the best for her chronic pelvic pain.

Taking a deep breath, I ran from the kitchen, past the dining room table, and into the living room where the couch was against the back wall. I stared at the impression on the left recliner. Then I shouted, "She isn't here!" My body shook uncontrollably. Tears began to pour down my face.

I left the living room, shuffling into the dining room and then the kitchen again, in and out of the rooms. "She isn't here!" I said again, and then over and over, now in a monotone, robot-like voice. The last time I'd been here was almost two weeks ago—September 28th, the day my daughter died. If I'd known that the pain she was having that day was different from all the other days, I might have been able to save her. That was almost the worst part.

My phone rang, snapping me out of this hypnotic state. It was Marty's brother, who lived next door. He must have noticed my car in the driveway and become concerned. I'm sure he remembered me standing by the porch screaming, "Don't ever make me go in that house again!" and Marty saying, "Don't worry. You won't have to."

I answered the phone, only because I knew that if I didn't, he might come down the hill and knock on the door. It was difficult to manage, but I got out the word. "Hello?"

"Deb, I see you're at the house," he said. "I just wanted to check on you."

I sobbed into the phone, "She isn't here. She isn't here." As if he, too, would find this information new and alarming.

I had picked out the clothes she'd worn for the private viewing. I had chosen the obituary picture. Marty, Brendan, and I wrote the eulogy. I sat in church during the funeral and placed a rose next to the urn at the cemetery that contained my daughter's ashes. Yet now, here I was roaming around her house for hours like a ghost, chanting, "She isn't here."

Part I

Chapter One

Elementary school teachers ask their students, "What do you want to be when you grow up?" I always wanted to say, "When I grow up, I want to be a mom." But I never said this out loud. No one else ever responded this way, so I didn't think it was an acceptable answer. I loved dogs, horseback riding, and swimming in the ocean, so when asked this question, my top three occupations were veterinarian, jockey, and oceanographer.

When I was ten years old, my parents asked my younger brother, Craig, and me to sit at the kitchen table because they had something important to tell us. My father announced, "Your mom is going to have a baby." I hugged my mom and hoped for a sister. The following June my wish came true when Krista was born.

About two years later, this exact scene at the kitchen table repeated itself. Months later, I got off the junior high bus and walked home to find my mother missing. This never happened, so I was scared. I called our neighbor who was a close family friend. She told me my mom had gone into labor while I was at school. Shawn surprised us by coming three weeks early and weighing just a little over four pounds.

Shortly after I turned fifteen, my parents had all of us gather around the kitchen table. Shawn was in a highchair, and Krista, now three, sat in a booster seat. My father said, "Your mother and I have something important to tell you." I thought, *You've got to be kidding, Mom can't possibly be having another baby.* Then he continued, "We're moving to Upstate New York."

Instead of staying seated for a family discussion, I quietly fled to the bedroom I loved and considered a second home. How could I leave my friends? For as long as I could remember, I'd been waiting to go to East Brunswick High School in New Jersey. The time had finally arrived. I was about to finish ninth grade; the high school was grades 10 through 12. Even though I hadn't started classes there, I was one of three freshmen already running on the varsity track team. Now my track career would be over.

My father was part owner of a lucrative and well-known sub shop in Edison, New Jersey. His produce man had told him about this little town in Upstate New York called Canajoharie. Our family had traveled there a few times, and my father had fallen in love with the cows wandering around in grassy fields, the views of only farmhouses for miles. In contrast, nothing about this town appealed to me. I'd have much preferred another sibling.

The sub shop took up most of my father's time. He worked over twelve hours a day and often on weekends. I didn't get to see him much. Even as a young child, I'd sit at the top of the stairs until I heard, "Here's Johnny!" on TV, which meant it was 11:30 on a school night. This was my cue that dad was home and most likely sitting on the couch eating peanut butter and jelly for dinner. I'd quietly come down the stairs. My mom wouldn't even be mad; she'd let me sit with him for a half hour watching *The Johnny Carson Show* before telling me to go back to bed.

The move was partly because my dad said he'd missed seeing Craig and me grow up, and he didn't want that to happen again with Krista and Shawn. He was tired of living a hectic life with work and the New Jersey traffic. Our new home would have fresh air, they told us. His childhood dream had been to live on a farm. Now, he would realize that dream, and we'd all come along, like it or not.

Bribery isn't a bad thing when you're on the receiving end. My parents said that when we moved, I could get a dog, which I hadn't been allowed to have in our East Brunswick home. On the farm, we'd also get a three-wheeler and a snowmobile. I had never ridden either of these, but it sounded like a fun thing to do. I would have first choice of bedrooms, even ahead of my parents. And the last item on the list was my very own horse. I was wary of starting life over in what appeared to be the middle of nowhere, but all these things made me willing to try.

A group of friends and I went to the mall for new school clothes. We wondered what girls in Canajoharie were wearing. I went into the dressing room while my friends handed me things I would never normally wear, saying, "Try this." We assumed girls living in a rural community wore western type clothing. I purchased several plaid skirts, some matching hush puppy sweaters, and a pair of tan cowboy boots with white stitching up the sides.

During the summer of 1982, we packed up everything from our suburban Jersey home. Then we drove to a farm in Palatine Bridge, the town neighboring Canajoharie. The first thing I did was go to the animal shelter and bring home a black lab mix puppy, who we named Pete. I had no idea what he was mixed with, but he had adorable white markings on his feet, chest, and nose. My parents followed through on all their promises. I selfishly picked the largest bedroom. A red three-wheeler and a black Ski-Doo snowmobile were parked in one of the outbuildings. Before I could get my horse, a woman who lived down the road was going to teach me how to take care of one. School was about to start. I was terrified to walk into a high school being the new girl in town.

That day arrived way too soon. I'd see my future husband that first day, although we weren't introduced, and I didn't know his name. Over forty years later, Marty still tells people, "I saw this girl with blonde hair and blue eyes walking down the stairs of the high school wearing a pair of cowboy boots." Turns out, this was not what girls in Canajoharie were wearing.

Being the new student in a high school that graduated less than a hundred a year had its problems. These boys and girls had known each other their whole lives. Not many people moved to this little town. There were girls smoking cigarettes in the bathroom. When I walked in, they called me a "bitch." In gym class, girls played volleyball with one goal in mind—to hit me in the face with a spiked ball. A girl violently shoved me into lockers as I was walking down the hall, ripping my shirt.

In 1982, there weren't anti-bullying laws. These girls didn't know me. I hadn't been there long enough to learn their names. The youth center across the street had a restroom I soon used to avoid the girls who were always in the school bathroom. Of course, many of the girls were kind and friendly. But these negative memories are the ones that stay with me. On extremely bad days, I'd get home from school and tell my parents, "When I turn eighteen, I'm out of here."

During a school vacation, I worked on a farm with horses. This brief experience made me think I was ready for horse ownership. My father paid a neighbor a few hundred dollars for a young brown horse named Cisco. It turned out Cisco didn't like people very much. He sometimes tried to bite anyone who came near him. This small problem did not deter me. I was convinced that with time, Cisco would love me, just like Pete the black lab from the animal shelter did.

There were beautiful fields behind our barn, with paths to ride. We were in one of those fields on a summer day when Cisco suddenly took off at a full gallop, with me in the saddle. When a horse is galloping, all four feet come off the ground together with each stride. I pulled back on the reins and yelled, "Whoa!" several times, but Cisco kept galloping. I wasn't aware that a horse could switch gears in an instant. One moment Cisco was at a full gallop, and the next moment he was perfectly still.

Physics tells us that an object in motion stays in motion. That object was me. I flew over Cisco's head and landed on the ground in front of him. Cisco turned and ran back towards the barn. Somehow, I wasn't injured, only had the wind knocked out of me. I walked home to find my mother standing near the barn doors looking horrified. She had watched Cisco race into the barn with an empty saddle. He wasn't the right horse for a beginner. More evidence that I wasn't qualified for horse ownership is that I still describe him as a young brown horse. I don't even remember what breed he was.

Eventually things at school improved, especially when I started dating Marty during my junior year. He was cute and funny, with curly brown hair and hazel eyes. People around Marty were always laughing. We were in gym class together. When we played volleyball, Marty and I made sure we were on the same team. We also stood next to each other in the rotation. Once we rotated to the front row, I'd set the ball so he could spike it. We weren't trying to hurt anyone, we just wanted to win.

Marty was the quarterback of the football team. One Saturday after a game, we both went to the same party and stayed together through the evening. We walked outside when my father pulled up in our 1978 cream-colored Oldsmobile. My grandfather was sitting in the passenger seat. He was visiting from New Jersey and had come along for the ride.

I motioned for my dad to put down the window. "Can we give Marty a ride home? It's on the way." Marty and I slid into the backseat. I thought it was funny that Marty, who had been talkative all night, didn't say a word from the moment he got in the car until we pulled into his driveway. As he got out, he said, "Thanks." It was November 19th. We still consider this first date our anniversary, even though we had only kissed.

The following Monday, I walked into the school cafeteria and sat down with Marty and his friends at their lunch table. From that moment on, we did everything together. Marty was an avid snowmobiler. With a group of riders, we'd get on the snowmobiles in the morning and ride all day long, stopping at different food places along the way to get warm. If we weren't snowmobiling on the weekend, we would be downhill skiing. Marty's parents had an in-ground pool in their backyard. During the summer we swam in the pool and at various lakes in the area. My mom started setting a place for him at our dinner table.

Marty was a year older than me. After high school graduation, he went to study computer science at Siena College, about an hour away. I felt lost during my senior year at school without him. Most weekends, he came home. We wrote each other letters and mailed them, then we'd see each other before the letters arrived. It was still comforting to go to the mailbox and read what he'd written.

When I graduated a year later, I decided to get a teaching degree. Being a mom someday was still a priority and foremost on my mind. This career choice was the best option to have a job and a family. I chose a school that was not far from Marty's college.

In February of my senior year of college, Marty and I went skiing in Lake Placid over a long weekend. When we pulled into the parking lot of our favorite restaurant, I noticed Marty was unusually quiet. He reached in the backseat to get something, and his hands were shaking. Sometime during the day, he must have bought a single red rose that was wrapped in green tissue paper. He handed me the rose and said, "Smell it."

I smelled the rose. "It smells nice," I said.

Marty repeated himself. "Go ahead and smell it."

Now I was confused. I held the rose closer and said again, "It smells really nice."

Marty's eyes grew wide. He grabbed the rose from my hands, looked at it, then started frantically tearing at the green tissue paper. Finally, from the bottom, he pulled out a diamond ring. Earlier, he'd carefully placed the diamond ring inside the rose petals, but it had fallen out.

I started to cry and said, "Yes."

Marty put the ring on my finger. To this day he says, "Technically I never asked you to marry me. You saw the ring and assumed."

We were married that summer, in 1988. I was only 22—young even for back then. I was interviewing at different school districts in the area because Marty and I wanted to stay near our families. My brother Craig was in college, but Krista was eleven and Shawn only eight. Marty had a job working with computers at a company close to where I now called home.

Before September, I got hired to teach second grade by the Canajoharie School District, where I would remain for the next 33 years. So much for "When I turn 18, I'm out of here." Most of the people I graduated with left Canajoharie. I'm the one who stayed.

After getting back from our honeymoon in Hawaii, Marty and I rented a little house. We were married for less than a month when I brought home a yellow lab puppy. I treated Cider like she was my first child. Within a short period of time, I had graduated from college, gotten married, moved into a new home, added a puppy to our lives, and started my teaching career.

Marty had become friends with a guy named Brian at his workplace, and one day he invited Brian and his wife, Patty, for a ride down the Mohawk River on our speedboat. It was a beautiful Sunday morning, sun shining, skies blue, the river calm. I don't use the word speed boat lightly. When Marty hit the gas, the front of the boat lifted into the air and then eventually leveled off. To stop required slowing down gradually or the boat would sort of collapse into the water. It was a small boat, with only a chair for the driver, a chair beside it, and then a bench-like seat along the back. Marty sat in the driver's seat with me next to him, Brian and Patty in the back seat.

Marty slowed as he approached the dock at the restaurant. Water suddenly poured into Brian's and Patty's laps. They jumped up, but it was too late.

"Well, that's a little cold," Brian said, but I could tell he wasn't angry.

Patty just laughed.

"I'm sorry," I said, horrified. "That sometimes happens—but not usually."

She and Brian just kept laughing and didn't mind eating breakfast in their wet underwear.

Then, on our way back up the river, the boat ran out of gas. Marty guided the boat to a grassy hill. He and Brian walked to a pay phone to call my brother. Patty and I sat on the grass.

Again, I apologized. "I feel like the worst hostess ever," I told her, but she just waved it all off.

We chatted while waiting for the guys to return. When they did, Marty had good news. Craig was home and soon showed up with a can of gasoline.

Our first attempt at entertaining as a married couple had failed miserably. That night I said to Marty, "I don't think we made a good impression. The next time we invite them to do something, they'll probably be busy." But instead, somehow, this day filled with mishaps was the beginning of a lifelong friendship. Soon we were hiking in the Adirondacks, camping at lakes, and having weekend game nights.

*　　*　　*

To save money for a down payment on a house, Marty and I briefly moved into a trailer on my parents' farm. I say "briefly" because the trailer was ungodly hot in the summer, freezing in the winter, and claustrophobic all the time. We used kerosene heaters as our main source of heat. Sometimes the kerosene ran out while we were sleeping. When we woke up, it was so cold we could see our breath. Other times the heater in a small, enclosed space turned our bedroom into a furnace. We'd wake up with parched lips and joke that we needed IV fluids. The trailer was on a hillside with no driveway. After a rainstorm, I'd have to floor my car's gas pedal and spin the tires to get up the muddy hill.

Marty and Brian played basketball with a group of guys one night a week. While they played, Patty came to the trailer so we could do exercise videos. I'd laugh when Patty got out of her car wearing rubber boots covered with plastic bags. With each step, her feet would get sucked into the mud and she'd struggle to get to the front door. We fondly called the trailer, "a tin can in rut valley".

I'd lie in bed at night listening to the wind howl and imagine what would happen if the trailer started rolling down the hill. Only our clothes hanging in the tiny closet were in front of our bed. I thought, *Maybe it won't be that bad, nothing sharp or heavy will fall on me.* We planned on living there a lot longer to save money, but one morning Marty woke up and said, "Find us a house."

It didn't take long to find the perfect starter home. The house was on a cul-de-sac with about 1200 square feet of living space. It had three small bedrooms and one full bath. The elementary school I worked at was literally two minutes away. We didn't care for the decor, but that gave us an opportunity to make it our own. It had paneling everywhere, brown carpeting, and a linoleum kitchen floor. Marty took down the paneling and painted the walls. We replaced the carpet and put a hardwood floor in the kitchen. It was still just the three of us, Marty, me, and Cider.

I saw my gynecologist for a yearly exam when I was 26. After some random testing, I sat in his office across from the giant "doctor" desk that all gynecologists seem to have. With no preface, he blurted out, "You're not ovulating. It could take years for you to get pregnant." I hadn't been trying to get pregnant. Marty and I didn't plan on starting a family for a few more years. But his words terrified me.

When I got home, I called my mom. Through tears I told her what the doctor said.

"Don't believe that doctor," she said. "Women in our family get pregnant without intending to." Her words were reassuring.

Still, this announcement by the doctor sent me into a full-blown panic. All I had ever wanted was to be a mom. Marty was hesitant, but we decided to move up our plans.

A month later, I told Marty I was pregnant. He was in shock. "But you said it could take years!"

I shrugged. "That's what the doctor said."

As a working mother-to-be, I was glad to have night nausea instead of morning sickness. For the first three months, I mostly ate cereal for dinner. Then the nausea subsided, and I had an easy pregnancy. From my first ultrasound, I was told my due date was April 10th.

On April 8th, I woke up with what I thought were back spasms. Then I realized the spasms were happening every ten minutes. The doctor's office said to wait until the contractions were closer to five minutes apart. But after an entire day, they never got closer together, so we went to the hospital. "Walking will help," a nurse told me. Even though I'd been awake for almost two days, I did lap after lap around the halls. The midwife showed me what looked like a crochet needle, which she used to manually break my water. Instantly I went into hard labor. It took about 48 hours to meet our baby girl—on exactly April 10, 1993. We named her Kelsey Marie.

Chapter Two

Kelsey was born with a headful of dark hair that stuck up in the middle like a mohawk. She had a round face, and a large dimple on her chin, which was common on my side of the family.

Right from the start, Kelsey cried a lot. I told myself not to worry, that all babies cry. The nursing books said not to give her a pacifier, so we didn't. But I did notice that when I turned on the vacuum cleaner, the humming sound often calmed her. This gave me an idea. I put a blank cassette in a tape recorder, turned on the vacuum cleaner, and pressed record. Then I left the vacuum on and recorded the sound for 30 minutes. The tape recorder became a necessity in the nursery. When I put Kelsey in her crib, I played the cassette as she fell asleep. I tell people that I created the first white noise machine.

I learned that doctors would call Kelsey a colicky baby. Colic is when a baby cries for a long time for no apparent reason. But one day, when Kelsey was two months old, and crying, I thought this cry was different. I pressed my lips against her forehead. She felt hot.

Someone had given me an ear thermometer at my baby shower, but I didn't anticipate needing it this soon. The directions said to press the power button, insert the cone-shaped end into the ear, and then press another button to get a reading. This seemed simple enough, but I hesitated because her ears were so tiny. As gently as I could, I inserted the thermometer into Kelsey's ear. The little gray box said 101 point something. Hoping I'd used it incorrectly, I repeated the steps only to conclude that Kelsey had her first fever.

To increase my first-time mom anxiety, it was a Saturday. There was a hospital not far from where we lived, but Marty and I decided to bring Kelsey to the hospital where she was born, because they would have her medical records. When we arrived, I expected to sit in the waiting room, but we were called into a room right away. Apparently a two-month-old with a fever deserved immediate attention.

The doctor examined Kelsey, looking for the common causes of a fever. She didn't have an ear infection, her throat looked normal, and her lungs were clear. The doctor pulled a sticker out of a drawer. "I'm testing her for a urinary tract infection," he told me. Then he placed the sticker over Kelsey's urethra and said, "Now we wait."

Eventually Kelsey peed, and some urine collected in the little pouch. It turned out she did have an infection. The doctor prescribed an antibiotic and sent us on our way, saying she should start to get better within 24 hours. The pharmacist made a liquid antibiotic and gave me an oral syringe.

I'd never given medicine to a baby. I drew the medication out of the bottle while carefully measuring the amount. Then, holding my breath, I pressed the plunger, which released the liquid into the side of Kelsey's mouth. Soon, this routine became much easier. The fever and urinary tract infection went away. But her colicky nature did not.

At a routine visit with the pediatrician, I mentioned that Kelsey cried a lot and seemed uncomfortable much of the time—though, as she was my first child, I didn't know what a normal amount of crying was. But my mother and mother-in-law both had a lot of experience and agreed that she often seemed in distress. The pediatrician prescribed a medication to help Kelsey digest her food, to be given 30 minutes before eating. I soon thought of this bright green liquid as a potion with magical powers, because Kelsey stopped crying.

When Kelsey had the urinary tract infection (UTI), she had a low-grade fever. But by the time she was six months old, very high fevers had become a regular part of our lives. Her temperature would be normal and then suddenly and rapidly climb to 104 degrees. The first noticeable signs were flushed cheeks and glossiness in her eyes. With time and experience, all I had to do was look at Kelsey to know she had a fever. I started referring to myself as the human thermometer.

Besides being worrisome, these quick high fevers were a challenge. When I gave Kelsey liquid acetaminophen to bring her temperature down, her gag reflex kicked in and she immediately vomited. Then I had to wait another four hours before attempting to repeat this process. Even if she kept the medicine down, her fever only lowered slightly, and only for a couple of hours, before shooting back up to 104. It would remain that high until I could give her another dose.

We developed a fever protocol. Kelsey's temperature would be over 104, usually spiking at night. Step one was to get off the footed pajamas that trapped in all that heat. Step two was to put her in the tub and sponge her off with cool water for about ten minutes. This usually lowered her fever enough to lessen my anxiety. Step three required getting fever reducing medicine to stay in her stomach. If I gave Kelsey the medicine before a bath, she was more likely to throw it up because of her high temperature.

Doctors told me that viruses were causing these high temperatures and gave me conflicting solutions. Some said to give her acetaminophen and then three hours later give ibuprofen. Other doctors said this plan might overload her liver, and it was better to have a high temperature than a liver trying to process too much medication. We settled on acetaminophen suppositories, which I hadn't known existed. She couldn't throw these up, and they were easier on her liver. There was still some controversy over these suppositories, because they don't release the medicine in a slow and steady fashion, but this was the method we decided to use because it worked best.

I always went into Kelsey's bedroom and checked on her before going to bed. One night I opened her door and found her listless body lying in a pile of vomit. When I lifted her from the crib, she was on fire. I got the thermometer and put it in her ear. The little gray box said, "Out of Range." I didn't know this was possible. An out-of-range temperature meant over 105. Maybe I should immediately have gone to the hospital, but my instincts told me to lower her temperature as quickly as possible. I began the fever protocol and sponged her down with cool water in the tub. This brought her temperature down to around 104. Medication then brought her temperature down a bit more.

The next day Kelsey's pediatrician ordered a chest x-ray and said she had pneumonia. I assumed she would be admitted to the hospital. He said, "The hospital is the worst place for a sick baby." I understand that now, but at the time, I was terrified to bring Kelsey home when her temperature was still going up to 105. Luckily, once the antibiotics got in her system, she started to recover.

Whenever Kelsey had a virus, she'd be sleepy and have a high temperature. But one night, around the age of two, she had a low-grade fever—which never happened—and she was screaming. The pediatrician tested her urine and said she had another urinary tract infection. I drove straight to the pharmacy and picked up the antibiotics. But antibiotics aren't magic, and after a few hours she was still screaming and appeared to be in serious pain.

My mother suggested we put her in the tub, thinking the cool water might make her more comfortable. This didn't work. Finally, Marty and I decided to put Kelsey in the car. We drove around for hours without a destination. As with many toddlers, the movement of the car soothed her, and eventually, she calmed down and fell asleep.

Shortly after this second UTI, I became pregnant. The doctor said my due date was May 20th. We asked Kelsey, now two and a half, what she wanted to name the baby. A Winnie the Pooh fan, she suggested

Eeyore. We called the baby Eeyore throughout my pregnancy. No longer a baby, Kelsey was now a little girl with blonde wavy hair to her shoulders and bright blue eyes that often brought compliments from strangers.

On May 19th, my sister called me at around 8:00 PM. "You know you're going to have that baby tomorrow," she said.

I laughed and reminded her that I was in labor with Kelsey for 48 hours.

She continued teasing me, "You're too organized and on time not to have that baby on May 20th."

I hung up the phone and continued watching a Tom Cruise movie. Less than an hour later, I had my first contraction. The contractions immediately felt different than they had with Kelsey—stronger, more intense. Still, I thought, *We probably won't need to go to the hospital until sometime tomorrow.* But about halfway through the movie, I told Marty, "I think we need to go now." I called my mother-in-law to come stay with Kelsey, who was asleep in her room. Marty and I left as soon as she arrived.

On the drive to the hospital, I was writhing in pain. "Drive faster," I said, though I didn't want Marty to panic. But I was starting to think I might have this baby in the car.

The nurse got us settled in a room. After checking me, she said, "I'll call the doctor in the morning."

I was confused. This was hard labor, was it not? For a few hours I suffered, until I couldn't take it anymore. Then I told Marty, "Go get the nurse."

The nurse came in to check on me. She looked startled and said, "Don't push! I need to get a doctor."

Brendan was born twenty minutes later, after only 7 hours of labor. When I held him in my arms for the first time, it felt unreal. How did this happen so fast? In a few hours, when the sun came up, I called my sister to tell her she'd been right. Brendan was born on May 20th, as if I'd written it on the calendar of things to do that day.

When we arrived home with Brendan in the car seat, Kelsey was waiting in the driveway. As soon as I lifted the carrier out of the car, she touched the handle and said, "Bring him inside." She kept her hand there as I walked, thinking she was helping me. Cider was barking loudly in the background. Kelsey said, "Cider waking baby up. Cider be quiet."

We walked up the stairs to the living room. That's when I saw the huge Welcome Home sign Kelsey had colored and hung on the wall. I set the carrier down on the sofa.

Kelsey sat beside the carrier and held out her arms. "Give him to me," she said. The moment I put him in her arms, she started singing Rock-A-Bye-Baby.

This whole time, Marty was holding the video camera. He said, "How do you like your new brother Eeyore?"

Kelsey said, "Let's call him Brendan."

I laughed, relieved. We had told Kelsey that if it was a boy, we would name him Brendan, but I thought she might persist in calling him Eeyore.

I didn't have to return to work until September. The summer flew by, a blur of feeding, diapering, and (not much) sleeping that I relished, not wanting it to end. When the new school year began, getting everyone out of the house was challenging—especially since we had only one bathroom. I'd get myself ready for work, get Kelsey and Brendan ready to start their day, and then Marty or I would drop them off at the babysitter's house. Two days a week, Kelsey attended a local nursery school. There she got to do her favorite activity: making art projects.

Occasionally, I'd be walking by the closed bathroom door and hear Kelsey in there saying, "Ow, ow, ow!" I'd ask her, "Are you okay?" She'd answer, "I'm good," and then run off and continue playing. I thought this was strange, but I wasn't concerned because she'd leave the bathroom smiling. What I didn't know at the time was that it burned for Kelsey to urinate even when she didn't have a UTI. She'd have the urge to go, feel pain as she went, and then go back to whatever she was doing. This was how it had always felt for her, so she thought it was normal.

My parents still had the farm. The four of us went there often for dinner. Kelsey called my parents Pop and Nanny. I'd walk her through the barn, and she'd go "moo" at the cows. Then the cows would moo back at her, which she found hilarious. When my father went out on the tractor, she liked to sit in his lap. He'd let her hold the steering wheel and pretend she was driving. If Kelsey was in the house and heard Pop coming back from the barn, she'd run and hide.

Pop would walk into the kitchen and say, "Where's my precious?"

Kelsey would wait a moment before jumping out from her hiding place and shouting, "Here I am!"

One night in November, my phone rang at 4:00 AM. The moment you hear that sound at that time, you know something is terribly wrong. It was my mother. "I'm at the hospital," she said. "Your father had a heart attack."

I called my mother-in-law to come stay with Kelsey and Brendan, and Marty and I went to the hospital. As we arrived, I saw my father being rushed by on a gurney and pushed into an ambulance. I didn't even have a chance to speak to him; he was being taken to a hospital 40 minutes away that had a cardiac catheterization lab.

Marty drove with my mom, Shawn, and me in the car. We rode in total silence. No one knew what to say. We were in shock. My father had just turned 55.

When we got to the hospital, Marty left to go find my sister. She was in her college dorm room 20 minutes away. I'm not sure how much time passed, but it seemed like only minutes later when the doctor came through the double doors into the waiting room and said, "I'm sorry. He didn't make it."

How had this happened? I wanted to run from the hospital, but the three of us sat back down. We had to wait for Marty to return with Krista. The moment they stepped off the elevator and saw our faces, they knew. We all held each other and cried.

Later that day, I wondered: How do I tell Kelsey that she'll never see Pop again? I walked into her bedroom. She took one look at me and said, "Mommy, why is your face so sad?"

I hesitated, not sure what to say.

"Tell me!" Kelsey begged. She was getting upset just by the sight of me. "Tell me why you're so sad."

I sat next to Kelsey on her bed. "Mommy is sad because Pop died this morning," I said. "Now Pop is in heaven."

"When people go to heaven, they never come back," Kelsey remembered.

Her response surprised me. I didn't expect a four-year-old to grasp what I was saying. She asked, "Is there food in heaven? Will Pop be thirsty? Did he remember to bring his flashlight?"

I tried to reassure her. "Heaven has everything that Pop needs."

Kelsey frowned and crossed her arms over her chest. "But I didn't get to say goodbye."

"I didn't either," I told her. "Let's say goodbye to Pop in our prayers."

We knelt on the floor beside her bed and said a prayer.

Then Kelsey looked up at me and asked, "But who will call me precious?"

I said, "We'll always remember that Pop called you precious. And those memories will make us sad for a long time. But then one day those memories will make us smile."

For the next few weeks, I went to the farm a lot to help my mom. I was concerned that Kelsey would get confused. Each time we drove over, I reminded her that Pop wouldn't be there.

One night I was sleeping when I heard Kelsey calling me, "Mommy! Mommy!"

I jumped out of bed and ran into her bedroom. She was sitting up in bed. She said, "When you first told me Pop was gone, I didn't believe you. Now I do and I miss him. Would you show me again how to talk to Pop?"

We put our hands together. I said, "You can talk to Pop anytime and anywhere you want to. Just say his name and tell him whatever you're feeling and thinking."

As the oldest sibling, I felt it necessary to take charge. Craig lived more than two hours away, Krista was in college, and Shawn was still in high school. There were cows in the barn that needed to be milked twice a day. I found someone to do that while we figured things out. My mother would have to sell the cows and the farmhouse. It wasn't possible for her to take care of the animals and 100 acres of land. I also needed to find her and Shawn a place to live. Everything about our lives had changed overnight.

Chapter Three

At nursery school graduation, Kesley was a head taller than her classmates. She looked grown up wearing a floor length lavender flowered dress. The children all wore graduation caps made from black construction paper that said "Class of 2011" in gold glitter. She proudly held her bouquet of yellow roses and baby's breath as she stood next to Marty and had her picture taken.

The best part about nursery school graduation was that Kelsey would start kindergarten in the fall. Nursery school was three hours a day and only two or three times a week. She was excited that kindergarten would be every day from 8:00 to 3:00. We went shopping, and along with a whole new wardrobe, she picked out a lunchbox, a backpack, and all the necessary school supplies.

Because I taught at the school Kelsey would be attending, she'd go to work with me—an extra bonus for both of us. As September got closer, she counted down the days until school started. She couldn't wait to meet her teacher and classmates. A big decision was what to wear that first day. She chose a blue jumper with a red top and asked me to braid her long blonde hair.

The day before school was to start, Kelsey began to feel the urge to urinate about every fifteen or twenty minutes. Each time, only a few drops came out, and it burned. Now that she was older, she could explain how she felt, and we knew this was the beginning of a urinary tract infection. We hurried to the doctor's office to get antibiotics, but also knew, with a sinking feeling, that there wasn't enough time. She was going to miss her first day of kindergarten.

That morning, I woke up and got dressed for school. "Mommy has to go to work," I reminded her.

"Please stay home with me," Kelsey begged. She started to cry, knowing everyone else would be at school today.

"I want to stay home, but I can't," I tried to explain. This was a difficult concept for a five-year-old to understand. "Nanny will stay with you. I'll be home as soon as I can." I tried not to let her see that I was desperately holding back my own tears. Crying in front of her would make this so much worse.

After pulling out of the driveway, I let myself cry—but only briefly, because the school parking lot was just minutes away. I sat in the car for a moment to collect myself, then glanced in the mirror. It was obvious I'd been crying, but the students wouldn't be here for another half hour.

When my second graders arrived, I smiled and greeted them the best I could. It was hard to focus, as all I could think about was Kelsey sitting home in pain instead of being in her kindergarten classroom. Another consuming thought: Would she be well enough to go to school tomorrow? I wasn't my best teacher self that day.

Happily for everyone, Kelsey was better and started kindergarten just one day late.

We started using the term "flare-up" when, for no apparent reason, Kelsey's burning urination became worse. She'd suddenly have awful pain that she said felt like fire. This pain made it impossible for her to walk afterwards—sometimes for minutes, sometimes an hour or more. A flare-up might last for a few days and then gradually subside. We learned that flare-ups were bound to happen and could occur at any time.

It was difficult to tell the difference between a flare-up and an actual UTI, so whenever Kelsey's pain increased, we went to the doctor. Kelsey would provide a urine sample, and the nurse would do a dipstick test in the office. Most of the time, the results showed a urinary tract infection, and the doctor prescribed antibiotics. (Now, I'm not convinced that antibiotics were always necessary during these visits.) Later, we became more adept at noticing the subtle differences between the two.

Kelsey hated it when a fever, a flare-up, or a UTI kept her from school. She worried that fun and exciting things were happening without her. Even though she missed school more frequently than most children, her schoolwork was exceptional, and she put significant effort into everything she did. At the end of many school days, Kesley would race into my classroom with important news to share. "I won a contest with my Smokey the Bear poster," she'd say, or "My story *The Snowman Hunt* won first place." Right from the start, teachers said she had advanced writing skills and was particularly creative with projects.

Every year, I saved anything I considered "special" that Kelsey or Brendan brought home. Then, over the summer, I'd make them each a scrapbook that included schoolwork, projects, and awards, as well as photos of them in their Halloween costumes and pictures from their birthday parties. One Christmas, Kelsey handed me a present. I opened it to find a scrapbook that began with photos of me as a baby through my years as a mom. Kelsey said, "You make scrapbooks for everyone else, but no one makes a scrapbook for you, so I did." She had enlisted the help of my mom to gather things from my life. The first page has the identification tag the hospital hung in my bassinet with a picture of a stork. Beneath it is the newspaper clipping that announced my birth.

Marty pulled me aside one evening. "You need to stay in bed tomorrow and not come out," he vaguely explained. The following morning, my bedroom door flung open as Kelsey, Brendan, and Marty yelled, "Surprise!" It was Mother's Day, and they had a breakfast tray filled with pancakes, scrambled eggs, toast, and a vase of fresh flowers.

This might not seem unusual; kids do special things for their moms on Mother's Day. But then Kelsey showed me her four-page description of how this Mother's Day breakfast would occur, with written directions and illustrations. She had divided up the tasks, so Marty and Brendan each knew exactly what part of the surprise they were responsible for. One drawing has a picture of Brendan waiting for the toast to pop with Marty standing at the stove scrambling eggs. Kelsey is arranging flowers, organizing presents, and pouring orange juice. Her directions state that Brendan needs to open the bedroom door because her arms are full. There is an illustration showing me lying in bed. On my nightstand, the digital clock displays their arrival time: 7:30.

At the beginning of fifth grade, Kelsey was planning her Halloween costume. That year she made herself into a fish tank. I gave her a very tall cardboard box, and she cut rectangles out from each side and painted it black. At a craft store, she picked out a bright blue fabric with different colored fish swimming around. The fabric was cut into four pieces and glued to the inside of the box. There was a hole in the top for her head and an armhole cut into each side. Some plastic plants that looked a bit like algae were glued to her tights, and she wore goggles, flippers, and a snorkel. After trick-or-treating, we went to the school gymnasium where everyone paraded around. Three winning costumes were chosen. Kelsey's came in first place. The newspaper article called her an aquarium.

For fifth grade graduation, students were asked to write a speech about how they would change the world, and Kelsey's was one of three chosen to be read at the ceremony. She stood at the podium and read her speech to an audience filled with students, teachers, and parents.

For years, members of the family would laugh and remind Kelsey that in her speech she said, "Why do kids in college need to drink beer instead of apple juice?"

Research tells us that creative people tend to be messy. They resist order and structure; they're often impulsive by nature. Their brains see the big picture, so they don't lose themselves in the small details. Kelsey was a creative person. She'd sit at her craft table for hours, leaving the art supplies strewn about instead of putting them back in the organizers I provided.

This caused problems between us because when I walked into her bedroom, all I saw was a disaster. I knew I wouldn't be capable of rational thought in such an environment, and I didn't understand how she could. But my daughter felt totally at home amidst the chaos, knowing exactly what result she wanted. She'd emerge from that messy room and give me beautiful cards for every occasion. She painted ceramics, made perfectly shaped animals from beads, and constantly drew, colored, and baked Shrinky Dinks. Looking back, I wish I hadn't nagged her so much to clean up her room and had respected our differences instead of trying to make her more like me.

Brendan's room was just the opposite of Kelsey's. He loved dinosaurs, army vehicles, and Power Rangers, which were all neatly sorted and organized in individual containers. My brother Craig once visited with his young son, who wandered into Brendan's room to play unsupervised. When we walked down the hall to see what he was up to, we discovered that he'd dumped all the containers into a huge pile in the middle of the floor.

Brendan's mouth fell open. He said, "I'm not cleaning this up!"

Craig knelt down and started scooping everything up and dropping armfuls of toys randomly into the containers.

Kelsey shook her head and laughed. "Oh no, Uncle Craig!" she said. "That's not going to work for Brendan."

"It will go a lot faster if we all work together," said my teacher-self.

Then we all got on the floor, including Brendan, who gave us specific directions as we sorted every toy into its correct bin.

Brendan was more of a math guy than an artist. He used to joke that it wasn't fair that Kelsey was ahead of him in school. When he turned in an art project, the teacher would often look a bit bewildered and say, "Kelsey is your sister?"

The two of them argued sometimes, just little stuff that I'd call normal brother and sister squabbles. Kelsey was always telling Brendan he was annoying. When my sister got engaged, we were meeting her fiancé's parents for the first time at a restaurant. On the way over, in the car, I said to the kids, "Don't sit next to each other, don't look at each other, and don't talk to each other."

Kelsey was confused. "But they're going to be a part of our family," she said. "Shouldn't we just be ourselves?"

I said, "Absolutely not!"

We had a wonderful lunch. Brendan and Kelsey sat at opposite ends of the table, as instructed. As we walked back to the car, I said, "Thanks guys! You did a great job."

*　　*　　*

Since the day we'd brought Kelsey home from the hospital, our yellow lab, Cider, had been a part of her life, and then a part of Brendan's. I remember initially being concerned that Cider would be jealous, since she'd been our only baby for her first five years. The parenting books told me to have Cider sniff something that had Kelsey's scent on it before they were introduced. I did this, but I don't think it was necessary. Cider welcomed Kelsey, and later Brendan, into our home. When Cider died of cancer at age twelve, none of us could stand coming home to an empty house instead of a wagging tail. I picked up a *Want Ad Digest* from a convenience store and saw that a litter of chocolate labs would soon be available.

On a Saturday morning, Kelsey had an event at school. We dropped her off and didn't tell her anything about our plans. Then Marty, Brendan, and I drove to the breeder's house in Saratoga. He showed us into his living room, where there were two female chocolate lab puppies. "I'll leave you alone for a bit while you choose," he said.

When he left the room, one puppy hid in the corner of a dog crate while the other puppy walked over to greet us. I said, "This one seems friendlier."

Marty said, "Why don't we take both of them?"

I laughed, assuming he was kidding. I'd never had more than one dog at a time and couldn't imagine how hard it would be to train two puppies. "You're kidding, right?" I asked.

Marty shook his head no. "Let's get both. Then the kids can each have their own puppy."

Still trying to process this idea, I somehow heard myself say, "Okay."

The breeder came back into the room. "How much would it cost if we took both of them?" Marty asked.

The breeder shrugged, smiled, "That would be great!" He gave us a slight discount, and off we went with two chocolate lab puppies in a cardboard box.

We picked Kelsey up from her event. I walked with her to our car, so I'd be next to her when she opened the door. As she started to climb into her seat, she saw the box. Her eyes grew wide. "Are these ours?" She reached into the box, gently petting each puppy, then laughed as the puppies responded by jumping up and licking her hand. We named the dogs Cocoa and Hershey.

Having two dogs instead of one turned out to be a wonderful idea. We had busy lives, and I felt less guilty when we weren't home because they had each other. They let the kids dress them in funny T-shirts and ballet tutus. When Kelsey had a Hawaiian-themed birthday party, they walked around wearing a lei and grass skirts. They were the best of friends, and they made us laugh every day.

The same year we got Cocoa and Hershey, Marty started a new career teaching at a local community college. His college degree from Siena was in computer science. Now, instead of working with computers in an office, he wanted to teach computer classes at the college level. To achieve this, he took classes at night until he got an MBA from the University at Albany. This new job had more flexible hours, which gave Marty the opportunity to become a football coach.

He started coaching fourth and fifth graders at Canajoharie, where his team played on the same field he'd played on in high school.

We had outgrown the starter house with one bathroom. On weekday mornings, we all needed to get ready for school and work. One person would be in the shower, another might need to use the toilet, and someone else would be trying to brush their teeth. Sometimes Brendan and I brushed our teeth at the same time. Usually, we had the correct rhythm of brushing and spitting in a synchronized fashion, but occasionally he'd spit on my hand or vice-versa. It was time to find a bigger house.

Finding a house that we liked in our school district was a challenge. We looked at more than a dozen properties. Finally, one day, our realtor showed us a house that would double our current living space. The property had 19 acres with a winding stream that went through the backyard. A little wooden bridge crossed the stream, leading to a pond filled with goldfish. Behind the pond was a forest with trails that curved around cascading waterfalls. After we toured the house, Marty and I sat on the front porch. "This house is perfect," Marty said.

"Really?" I didn't understand his enthusiasm, because all I could see was pink. Pink front door, pink living room, pink mantle…even the knobs on the kitchen cabinets were pink. The house also had white carpeting everywhere, which I thought was a terrible idea with two children and two chocolate labs. I shared my list of complaints.

"We can paint the house," he said. "And remove the carpeting."

His words made sense. I started to see the house in a new way. We could change the pink decor to more earthy colors and replace the carpeting with tile and hardwood floors.

Before making an offer, we brought Kelsey and Brendan over. The owners were there as we walked around. They had a hamster roaming about inside a hamster ball. Soon, a little white dog followed us everywhere. When we got in the car, I asked the kids what they thought. Kelsey was thrilled at the prospect of having a much larger bedroom. Brendan, who was seven at the time, asked, "Do the dog and hamster come with the house?"

We placed an offer. As soon as it was accepted, I became excited. We would leave our too small home in the village, surrounded by neighbors, and have a big home in the country with three large bedrooms, two full baths upstairs, and a half bath downstairs. The master bedroom had a walk-in closet, the huge kitchen a vaulted ceiling. There was a fireplace, a formal dining room, and an office the size of my previous bedroom. The yard was like living on a manicured golf course, and the woods—like a forest—were magical.

Moving in during summer vacation was ideal. In the morning, the kids and I crossed the wooden bridge to the pond. Cocoa and Hershey swam. Kelsey waded in the pond wearing water shoes, while Brendan watched for salamanders and frogs. It was the beginning of our new life.

But Kelsey's urinary problems were still a nuisance. They caused her pain and randomly interfered with our plans. Still, her school report card had straight A's and she played sports all year round, even in the summer. Her social calendar was full every weekend with friends and fun things to do. She had outgrown having viruses with high fevers. Some doctors thought she would also outgrow these urinary tract infections. That is what we believed and hoped for.

Chapter Four

What my family missed most about New Jersey was the ocean. Going to the Jersey shore for a week became our annual summer vacation. I'd plop my beach chair right in front of the water so I could more easily watch Kelsey and Brendan.

"Where are my goggles?" Kelsey would ask.

As soon as I handed them to her, she'd run into the water, where she'd spend the rest of the day. All you'd see was her floating among the waves with her face in the water. By the time we left, she'd have deep red lines where the mask had been.

When Kelsey was eleven, she got her period. That first summer we were lucky, and her period didn't coincide with our trip. The following year, though, I did the math and realized she'd likely have it while we were at the shore. Swimming in the ocean was her favorite thing to do, and she had never used a tampon before, so one morning I explained to her how they work. Then I left her alone in the bathroom, waiting nearby to see how it would go.

She came out almost immediately, looking worried. "When I press the tampon against my skin, it hurts," she said.

I nodded. "That's okay. It might hurt a little at first, but with practice you'll get used to it. Why don't you give it another try?"

She went back into the bathroom, but this time came out even more upset. "It doesn't hurt just a little, Mom. Trying to put the tampon in is really painful."

I didn't want to force the issue. "We'll try some other time."

Kelsey looked at me like she had no intention of ever trying this again. The pain she described concerned me, so I made an appointment for her to see a gynecologist. On the car ride there, she was incredibly nervous. Most 12-year-olds aren't subjected to a pelvic exam.

"This is embarrassing," she said. "I don't want to talk to him. You tell him what happened."

Dr. Benson came into the room and introduced himself to Kelsey. She was already on the exam table in a gown.

"Kelsey tried to use a tampon for the first time," I explained. "She said it really hurt when the tampon touched her skin."

When Dr. Benson inserted the speculum, Kelsey practically flew off the table. She was squeezing my hand as she tried to stay still.

"I am not hurting you," the doctor said firmly.

"Ow, ow, ow!" Kelsey said, writhing in pain.

"I am not hurting you," he said again, this time louder.

Tears were pouring down Kelsey's face. The exam was fast—maybe a minute or two. Still, I don't know why it didn't occur to me to tell Dr. Benson to stop. I was kind of in shock by his behavior, and I thought that, in the end, he might find a reason for her pain. To this day, I feel guilty about that. But Kelsey told me much later that she'd always blamed the doctor, not me.

We left with no explanation for her symptoms. He seemed to think she was being dramatic and overreacting. These aren't his words; it was just the impression we both got. Kelsey suffered for days after this physical exam.

I had chosen Dr. Benson because he was my gynecologist—not the same one who had told me I wasn't ovulating. He had delivered Brendan. I'd known and trusted him for more than ten years. He was always kind, easy to talk to, and well known in our area. Of course, I never went back to him. Now we both needed to find a new doctor.

Kelsey's next appointment was with a urogynecologist—a doctor with special training to treat women with pelvic floor disorders. He recommended that Kelsey try a type of biofeedback designed to retrain the pelvic floor muscles by either strengthening the muscles or learning to relax them. At biofeedback appointments, Kelsey had to insert a probe just like you would insert a tampon. Inserting the probe hurt and exacerbated her symptoms. Eventually, we gave up and accepted the fact that she couldn't use tampons.

Kelsey's flare-ups continued causing life to be interrupted without warning. We typically did the Jersey shore trip with my side of the family, but a few times we went with Marty's two brothers and their families. This meant Kelsey and Brendan got to spend time with their four cousins who were all close in age.

On one such trip, the plan was to go to Great Adventure and spend the day riding roller coasters, the log flume, and any ride that spins. When morning came, Kelsey peed, and a horrible burning pain took over. Everyone left for Great Adventure while I stayed with her at the hotel. She was in agony all day long and crying for two reasons. The pain, yes—but also, just like that first day of kindergarten, she was terribly sad. Her family was having fun without her. Two of her cousins lived in a different state, and she got to see them only once a year. These were special moments of her life that she'd never get back.

During softball season, we noticed that Kelsey had more burning pain than usual. It took us years to realize the cause: those gray polyester pants with fitted ankles didn't allow for any air flow. Many times, she walked out of the dugout, found me in the stands, and whispered, "My bottom is on fire, and I can't take it anymore." She always used the word "bottom" because she thought other words were embarrassing. We'd leave in the middle of a game. Later we got permission for her to wear black athletic shorts instead of polyester pants, and her symptoms improved during softball season.

I don't remember how old Kelsey was when she started lashing out and blaming me for things that went wrong in her life. It was usually over silly stuff. If she was getting ready to go somewhere, she'd ask, "Where's my favorite purple top and the necklace that goes with it?" When I didn't know the answer, she'd get mad and start yelling at me. After a shower, she'd say "I need to put mousse in my hair before it dries. Where's my mousse?" I wasn't hiding her clothes, taking her jewelry, or stealing her hair mousse. For some reason, she thought I should know where all her things were. Kelsey misplaced things all the time, and again it was somehow my fault. "I left my volleyball jersey on the bleachers. Why didn't you notice?" She always felt guilty after an argument and apologized.

Marty would ask, "Why do you let her treat you that way?"

I always responded, "She's mad at the world and knows I'm the one person who will take it and love her no matter what." Maybe I didn't handle it in the best way possible, but this was the cycle that perpetuated itself. I showed Kelsey unconditional love, which is what I think a mother should do. And I'm sure the fact that she suffered so much made me more forgiving than I might have been.

Kelsey was long accustomed to the burning when she peed, but when high school started, a new symptom began. The burning pain started to linger after she urinated. This was different from a flare-up because a flare-up had a beginning and an end. This new prolonged pain was happening on a regular basis, sometimes burning for hours. The pain was random and unpredictable. Now her urinary symptoms started impacting everything she needed and wanted to do.

Prior to this new symptom, Kelsey had excellent school attendance and was absent only when she had a flare-up or a UTI. Now, though, she was missing classes regularly—especially morning classes. She'd wake up for school, go to the bathroom, and then be in excruciating pain. If she peed during the school day, she'd end up in the nurse's office. There wasn't anything the nurse could do; Kelsey just needed some place to stay until the pain subsided enough for her to walk normally, since, when it burned, she had to walk with her legs spread apart. "I don't want everyone to see me waddling around like a duck," Kelsey would tell me. Many days she needed to go to the bathroom by midday but would hold it until school was over to avoid problems.

Art was Kelsey's favorite class, and a guaranteed A on her report card. In eighth grade, students were asked to design a mock cover for the school yearbook. Kelsey made a geometric pattern using overlapping circles of various sizes. The circles were black and gold, because those were the school colors, and she added white circles for contrast. Her design was chosen and became the 2006-2007 yearbook cover.

The semester after this lingering pain began, art was the first class on her schedule. After the first quarter of her sophomore year, Kelsey handed me her report card. "Mrs. Reid gave me an F," she said with a mixture of anger, sadness, and disappointment. She was in shock that the art teacher would do this to her.

I was just as shocked. Including middle school, Kelsey had gotten an A in art for the last 12 semesters. Going from consistent A's to an F didn't make sense.

I called the teacher and asked, "Why was Kelsey given a failing grade on her report card?"

"She missed a lot of classes," said Mrs. Reid. She seemed annoyed by my question. "And her projects aren't finished."

"Kelsey has urinary problems," I explained. "When she goes to the bathroom in the morning, it burns when she pees. Sometimes it takes hours for the pain to go away."

The teacher didn't seem to care. "Her projects aren't finished, so she failed."

"Could you give her an incomplete?" I asked. "Then give her more time to finish the projects. I know she wants to."

"No," said the teacher, now sounding angry instead of just annoyed. "If she doesn't do the work during the semester, she fails." When I continued trying to explain that Kelsey was missing her class because of a medical problem, Mrs. Reid hung up on me.

Stunned, my next call was to the principal. I relayed this conversation to him.

There was a pause. Then he said, "I'm sorry, but the teacher decides whether to give a grade or an incomplete at the end of each semester."

I was furious. Not only that Kelsey's history of straight A's didn't matter, but also that they could be so lacking in compassion.

Holidays, vacations, birthdays, and special events became worrisome instead of joyful. Sometimes Kelsey could participate, other times she could not. Even when she wasn't in pain, the fear was always there. When Kelsey entered the bathroom, I felt anxious and a bit terrified. I didn't know if she'd walk out okay or end up writhing in pain on the bathroom floor.

When the latter occurred and the pain didn't subside in a reasonable amount of time, I'd take her to the emergency room. She'd crawl into the backseat of my car and try to balance herself on all fours, in too much pain to sit. Often, for the entire ride to the hospital she'd scream. I'd drive as fast as I could, crying myself as I listened to her pleas for help. It felt like torture.

When we arrived, though, we'd often be left in the waiting room. One time, while we waited, Kelsey was asked to be quiet because she was crying too loudly. Another time she was lying on the floor screaming, and a nurse walking by stepped over her. Sadly, from our experiences, we concluded that some people in the medical field become indifferent to seeing people in pain. For them, it's just another day at work.

When she was finally called into a room, they'd give her morphine intravenously. Her level of pain would improve almost immediately—a huge relief to both of us. Still, none of the doctors we encountered would prescribe at-home pain killers for a teenager, so we had no choice but to go to the hospital each time, especially since these events usually occurred at night. The emergency room doctor would send us home with a prescription for an antibiotic, always just assuming Kelsey had a UTI.

Many times, I went to work after being up all night in the emergency room. If we got home by 4:00 AM, I stayed awake, thinking it would be harder if I slept for a couple of hours. Usually that first day wasn't bad because my adrenaline was still flowing. It was the second day that I struggled. If I was sick, I'd go to work. I made sure that all my sick time was saved for Kelsey.

The lack of guidance we were getting from doctors was extremely frustrating. One morning, I sat at the computer and started researching medical conditions that caused painful urination. I'd been researching for hours when I came upon an article about something called vulvodynia. The description fit Kelsey perfectly, to the point that I knew without a doubt this was what she had. Why had no doctor ever mentioned this to us?

Now that I had a name for this condition, I needed to find a specialist. There was a gynecologist in Manhattan that was well-known for successfully treating patients with vulvodynia. I made an appointment for Kelsey to see him. It was the first time I'd felt hopeful in a long time.

The question was how to get to Manhattan. Kelsey and I had visited New York City many times—for Broadway shows, trips to the Statue of Liberty or Times Square. We'd ice skated in Central Park, and we loved to shop. But we'd always been with people who knew how to get around the city; all I had to do was follow them. I had seen firsthand how people drove on Manhattan streets, with cars, taxis, and buses swerving from lane to lane and then suddenly stopping. There was no way I'd drive a car in such an environment. I needed a plan, not to mention some courage to do this on my own.

When the day of the appointment arrived, I drove to a bus station in Ridgewood, New Jersey used mostly by people who worked in the city. I was warned to get there early because parking spaces went fast—so we did. Once I parked the car, I felt like phase one of our mission was complete.

From inside a tiny white trailer, a woman was selling bus tickets. I bought two round-trip tickets, and we waited in line along the curb, then boarded a bus to New York's Port Authority Bus Terminal. On arrival—Port Authority is a huge and confusing place—we just followed the people, and eventually found our way outside. Step two achieved. I hailed a taxi—something I had never done—and gave the driver the address. Step three. Almost there. I looked at my watch and let out a sigh of relief. We were going to be at the appointment on time.

Standing in the doctor's office at the check-in desk, I felt an enormous sense of accomplishment. I also felt optimistic for Kelsey. For so long we'd been searching for answers.

Soon we were called into a room. I turned around to give Kelsey some privacy while she put on a gown. She always asked me to stand at her head and hold her hand while she was being examined. I couldn't wait to meet the specialist and hear what he had to say.

"Do you think he'll use that speculum thing?" Kelsey asked, remembering her traumatic experience with the first gynecologist.

"We'll tell him not to," I assured her. "He's a vulvodynia specialist. He'll know what to do."

I had shared with Kelsey the research I'd done and how convinced I was that she had vulvodynia. I didn't tell her about the comments I'd read made by women with this condition. One woman said vulvodynia won't kill you, but you'll want to die. Another woman said it felt like there was a blowtorch between her legs.

"You do the talking," Kelsey told me. She always felt embarrassed, especially since all the doctors we'd encountered so far had been men.

Dr. Gibbons came into the room. He already knew why we were here. "Kelsey tried to use a tampon when she was twelve," I explained. "She said it hurt. Ever since then, everything we've tried, like biofeedback, has only made her symptoms worse."

Dr. Gibbons nodded, then asked Kelsey to lie back on the table. Then he held up an ordinary Q-tip. "I'm going to use this Q-tip to go around your vulva area like a clock, starting at 12:00," he said. "You tell me when it hurts."

As he pressed on various areas, Kelsey told him when it hurt a little and when it hurt a lot. During the exam, she had severe pain in multiple locations. When the doctor finished his exam, he asked her to get dressed and meet him in his office.

We sat across from Dr. Gibbons, and he did his best to explain in layman terms his opinion. "Kelsey has a subtype of vulvodynia called primary vestibulitis," he said. (Today, doctors use the term "primary provoked vestibulodynia"). "Your pain, Kelsey, is mostly at the entrance to the vagina, known as the vestibule. Since you first noticed this pain when trying to insert a tampon, we call it primary, which means since birth. The best treatment for the congenital form is a vestibulectomy. During this procedure, I would surgically remove the painful tissue. The surgery has a long and painful recovery but is the best option for women born with vestibulitis. You could try conservative treatments, but they don't usually work for the congenital form."

We left the appointment feeling vindicated. Kelsey wasn't alone. What she'd been experiencing for years had a name, and there were other women out there suffering just as she was. The doctor had validated her feelings.

Still, Kelsey was scared. Words like "long" and "painful" had caught her attention. "That surgery sounds awful," she said.

I agreed. The thought of surgically removing her vestibule sounded terrifying. "We need to learn more about vulvodynia and consider our options," I said. "Don't worry. We aren't going to rush into surgery."

The National Vulvodynia Association (NVA) reports that 16 percent of women will experience a type of vulvodynia at some point in their lives—though it's believed that the actual number is probably higher because women are too embarrassed to talk about it even with their doctor. Most women, even to female friends, aren't going to say, "Sorry I canceled our plans, but my vagina was on fire." Cleveland Clinic has the percentage slightly higher than 16 percent, saying that 1 in 4 women are likely to experience a type of vulvodynia during their lives.

It was 2009. Kelsey was 16. Over the last four years, we had explained her history to gynecologists and urologists. These doctors had witnessed the amount of pain she was in during pelvic exams, yet not one of them had ever mentioned vulvodynia as a possibility. The NVA reports that 60 percent of women with vulvodynia see three or more doctors before getting an accurate diagnosis. Many women, like Kelsey, consult doctor after doctor looking for answers while they suffer with life-altering pain. The process of getting a diagnosis can take years.

After meeting with Dr. Gibbons, I read every article and research paper I could find about vulvodynia, especially the primary type. Vulvodynia (pronounced vul-vo-DIN-ee-a) is defined as chronic pain in the vulva region, with no apparent cause, that lasts for three or more months. While the doctor used the word primary to describe Kelsey, other women may acquire vestibulodynia later in life. The acquired type is referred to as secondary and means that the patient formerly was pain free.

Provoked means the pain is caused when pressure is put on the vestibule, from a pelvic exam to prolonged sitting to sexual intercourse to even tight-fitting clothes. Women describe the pain as a burning, stinging, throbbing, or stabbing sensation in their vestibular area. Most notable is that this condition causes painful urination. When I read this, I felt both victorious and sad.

I researched success rates of vestibulectomies, which seemed to vary tremendously depending on the doctor and where the procedure was performed. This was not a common surgery, and at the time, didn't even have a CPT code—codes that are used across the country so doctors have a common language to identify all medical procedures and services. I read nightmare stories about women who had vestibulectomies with gynecologists who didn't specialize in this procedure. Dr. Gibbons told us his personal success rate was about ninety percent, and that people came from all over the world for him to do their surgeries.

Females with vulvodynia look like perfectly healthy women. I found websites where women with this condition shared their stories. One woman said she wished she had cancer instead of vulvodynia. People rally around people with cancer. Whole communities show them compassion and emotional support. In contrast, women with vulvodynia hide and often feel ashamed, even though the condition is something they have no control over. Many women expressed frustration because their own families didn't understand why they couldn't live normal lives. A common theme was women who got married and then divorced because sex for them was painful.

Our first medical trip into the city on our own had been a success; we had been treated well and understood. We now felt wiser and much better informed. But we also felt overwhelmed. I considered Kelsey's having the surgery to be a last resort.

Chapter Five

When Kelsey became a junior, it had been a year since we first met Dr. Gibbons. During that time, she was seeing other vulvodynia specialists—two in Manhattan and one in Rochester, NY. Getting a second, third, and even fourth opinion seemed necessary.

We implemented conservative treatments. Kelsey wore only underwear that was one-hundred percent cotton. Her underwear was washed separately from all other clothing, in hypoallergenic detergent. We switched to unscented toilet paper, and she wore unscented pads when she got her period.

Lidocaine is sometimes prescribed for women with vulvodynia. It is a topical gel that contains an anesthetic. The anesthetic causes numbness in the vulva area. When Kelsey tried applying lidocaine, it burned like the products you would put on a sore muscle. Applying gel that caused burning when her vestibule was already on fire was a terrible idea.

For nerve pain, she also tried a topical compounded cream—multiple medications combined by a pharmacist—and oral prescriptions. But as Dr. Gibbons had predicted, conservative treatments weren't making a difference in Kelsey's symptoms. She still had burning urination, flare-ups, and UTIs.

One morning, in October, it was raining lightly when Kelsey, Brendan, and I got in the car to leave for school. Our home on Brower Road had a gravel driveway that was as long as a football field. As I slowly drove away from the house, I noticed a dog on our front lawn approaching our moving car. I stopped, concerned he might walk in front of the car while it was still moving. Instead of continuing across the driveway, he jumped on my driver's side door and looked at me through the window. We stared at each other for a moment. He was a yellow-colored dog who looked to be part lab. I needed to get to work, and the kids needed to get to school, but this wasn't normal dog behavior. I thought, *Maybe this guy needs help.*

"Wait here," I told Kelsey and Brendan as I opened the car door. The dog eagerly followed me back to the garage. He didn't resist when I put a collar and leash over his neck, but then he refused to take a single step. I slipped off the leash and went into the house to get some food and water. He gently ate food from my hand. It was then that I noticed his ribs were protruding and several ticks were in his fur. With food and water in my hands, I coaxed the dog to follow me into our backyard kennel, which had two doghouses, a wooden floor, and a mesh roof. This was a safe place for him to stay until I got home.

I hurried back to the car, thankful that the rain was light and only my hair was damp. Now, without a doubt, the kids and I were going to be late for school. Kelsey would be home first. "He's in the kennel," I told her. "Stay away from him until I get home." My plan was to go house to house after work and hopefully find his owner.

When I got home, the outdoor kennel was empty, and Kelsey's car wasn't in the driveway, so I called her. "I sat with him in the kennel," she said. "He's such a sweet dog. I put him in my car and we're at a friend's house."

Kelsey didn't always do what I asked. "Send me his picture," I told her.

We lived on a rural country road. Checking with neighbors meant driving around in a car, not walking. I stopped at houses, knocked on doors, and showed people his picture. It didn't take long for someone to recognize the dog and tell me who his owner was.

When I went to this neighbor's house, a short stout man answered the door. I held out my phone and said, "This dog was in my yard this morning. Is it your dog?"

He squinted as he looked at my phone. "That looks like my dog, but my dog is in the backyard,"

"Maybe we should go check," I suggested.

The man remained in the doorway. It took some convincing for him to follow me down the porch steps and walk around the side of the house. We stood in his backyard. There was a dog chain lying on the ground, but no dog in sight.

He said, "Maybe it is my dog."

"What's his name?" I asked.

The man answered, "Chino, like cappuccino."

I called Kelsey and told her his name. I heard her say, "Chino, Chino," with a high-pitched, excited voice. Then she came back on the phone and said, "Mom, I really don't think this is their dog. He didn't even move when I called his name."

I believed this was the man's dog, so I asked him for their phone number. It was late, and Kelsey had the dog at someone's house about thirty minutes away. I apologized and said I'd call tomorrow. The man didn't seem the slightest bit concerned that a stranger had his dog.

The next morning a woman answered the phone. I said, "We have Chino. Come over anytime."

Minutes later, I heard a car coming down the driveway. A woman and her twelve-year-old son got out of their car. I opened the garage door, expecting the dog to run to his family. Instead, he turned right and walked into the bushes along my property.

The mother said, "He's probably just going home." The bushes were in the direction of her house. They got in their car and left.

The moment their car exited the driveway, the dog came out of the bushes, as if he'd been just waiting for them to leave. I called the mother and told her the dog was still in my yard. This time, she and her son came with a big, heavy chain. They put the chain on the dog and put him in their car. I was certain I'd never see him again.

Within a couple of hours, he was sitting in front of my garage looking at me. They came and got him again, but almost immediately he was back. He must have run to my house as soon as they let him out of their car. This time when I called, the mother was angry. "The kids aren't taking care of him like they said they would," she explained. "Just keep him." Then she hung up the phone without giving me a chance to respond.

I couldn't believe what I'd just heard. I didn't want their dog. When he'd briefly stayed at my house, I'd kept him separated from Cocoa and Hershey, who were now nine. The sisters made it clear that they didn't want another dog joining the family, and I truly didn't want a third dog. Kelsey had already named him Marley after the singer Bob Marley. She was crazy about this dog and begged me to keep him.

"Don't even think about it," I told her. "We are not having three dogs in the house."

Whenever Marty was exposed to a new dog, he had an allergic reaction. His eyes would swell, and he'd get congested. After a few nights of not being able to breathe, he said, "You have to find a home for that dog."

The next day, Kelsey noticed that the dog she called Marley had fleas. I was still calling him "the dog" because I knew giving him a name was a bad idea. Marty already wasn't happy about this situation. I asked everyone I worked with if they wanted a dog or knew of anyone who might be interested, but I wasn't having any luck.

In the meantime, my goal was to take care of this flea problem and not mention it to Marty. Kelsey kept the dog in the garage while I hurried to the store for flea shampoo. Marty had football practice and often stayed late at school talking to players and other coaches.

When Kelsey heard my car, she brought Marley out to the driveway. It was 8:00 PM and getting colder by the minute. We had our winter coats on as we lathered him up, using water from the garden hose. The directions said to leave the shampoo on for five minutes before rinsing. It was almost time to rinse when Marty pulled in. I knew shampooing the dog in the dark on a cold night would seem suspicious.

Marty got out of his truck. "What are you guys doing?" he asked.

Kelsey said, "We decided he needed a bath."

"He got a little muddy," I added.

Marty walked into the house looking unconvinced by our story.

Weeks went by, and I still hadn't found a family willing to take "the dog." During this time, predictably, we all fell in love with Marley. Soon enough, I caved and told the kids he could stay.

Kelsey was relieved and excited. As with our previous dogs, once Marty was exposed to him for a while, his allergies subsided. I took Marley to the vet to get the required shots and asked him how old he thought Marley was. The vet guessed about a year.

Marley immediately put on weight, which he desperately needed. It didn't take long for his body to fill out so you no longer saw his ribs.

He was now a beautiful dog that looked like a yellow lab mixed with a German Shepherd.

The next problem to solve was that Cocoa and Hershey wanted nothing to do with Marley. My first idea was to use a baby gate to keep Marley on one side of the house and the girls on the other. The moment I put the gate in the doorway, Marley leaped over it from a standstill and innocently stood between them. I grabbed Marley before the girls had a chance to lunge at him. Next, I put barstool chairs on each side of the gate to block Marley from jumping. That worked, and the house stayed divided for months. Every time we went from one side of the house to the other, we had to climb over those tall chairs. The silver lining: My thigh muscles were more muscular than if I'd actually exercised.

Marley just wanted to be friends, but Cocoa and Hershey weren't the slightest bit interested. We took the three dogs on walks together. Sometimes we put Marley in front so the girls could get close enough to sniff him. Then we switched places and put the girls in front. At night, we sat in the living room with their leashes on which forced Cocoa and Hershey to tolerate his presence. I wanted them to practice being in the same room and peacefully coexisting. Cocoa would lie on the floor, growl at Marley, and show him her teeth. I'd point my finger at her mouth and firmly say, "No!" Then she'd stop growling but lift her lip just enough so Marley could see that her teeth were still showing.

Marley made it clear to the girls that he wasn't challenging their authority. From the start, he was laid-back and patient. He never reacted negatively when the girls tried to show they were in charge.

Because he had such a calm demeanor, eventually Cocoa and Hershey accepted him into the family. After that, it turned out that having three dogs in the house wasn't much different from having two—and even better. I was now glad that when I'd tried to find Marley a home, no one had offered to take him. We were the lucky ones, because Marley had chosen us.

Years later, we laughed and shared with Marty the reason for that mysterious bath on a cold dark night. Marty always believed that when Kelsey said, "Chino, Chino," he, of course, knew his name but ignored her on purpose. "Me no Chino," Marty would say using a funny, deep voice he imagined Marley to have.

Dogs are fiercely loyal to their pack, but they usually choose someone to be their leader. Marley chose Kelsey. Maybe he understood that she was responsible for saving him. Her bedroom was his bedroom, and they slept side by side. When she opened her passenger side door, Marley jumped in, happy to be her copilot. Kelsey was always posing next to him, saying, "Take our picture." Marley gave Kelsey the unconditional love she desperately needed. He didn't care when she missed classes or had to stop playing sports. If she was sad and depressed about her circumstances, she'd curl up next to Marley and feel loved.

Chapter Six

I was with my students one day when my classroom phone rang. I was surprised that it was one of Kelsey's teachers calling me while I was working. "I think Kelsey is faking her pain and missing classes on purpose," said Miss Nolan.

My hands started shaking and my cheeks felt hot, but I was standing in front of a room full of seven-year-olds, so I fought to stay calm. "You have no idea what our lives are like," I said, quietly. "Kelsey lives in pain and is doing the best she can." I hung up before I lost control. This comment, from someone who couldn't possibly understand what we'd been through, was infuriating. It was also unprofessional to say this to me while I was working. I was a teacher, but also a parent. She wouldn't have called another parent during their workday. I had to turn around, face my second graders, and continue our lesson.

A friend who worked at the school suggested that Kelsey should have a 504 Plan. At the time, I didn't know what she was talking about. I soon learned: A 504 Plan is a federal law that protects the rights of individuals with disabilities in places that receive federal financial assistance and ensures that students with disabilities can get special accommodations to participate in school.

Dr. Gibbons submitted a letter to the school explaining that Kelsey's medical condition was interfering with her education. I met with teachers and administrators to create a list of accommodations that were written into an official document. The most important one was that Kelsey would have extended time to complete assignments when she was absent. If a semester ended, and Kelsey owed assignments, she would be given an incomplete and have time to turn in the work after the semester ended. This plan ensured that what happened to her in art class would never happen again, and we felt a sense of relief once it was put in place. Now, when she was absent, we didn't need to panic and be filled with dread.

As winter came to an end, it was time to start planning for Kelsey's junior prom. She tried on more than a dozen gowns; once she found the perfect dress, she shopped for jewelry and shoes. Hair and nail appointments were made. As the prom got closer, I became more and more nervous. What if after all these preparations, Kelsey had a bad night and couldn't go? She'd be devastated.

When the day of the prom arrived, Kelsey made it to her hair and nail appointments. Her wavy, blonde hair was swept into a bun with ringlets framing her face. Her dress, floor-length, had a heart shaped neckline, and was asymmetrical at the waist. The top had multi-colored shiny sequins. The bottom half was draped with a teal-colored satin fabric that had an ombre effect. All these details on the dress, and jewelry, brought out her bright blue eyes. She was happy, excited, and looked gorgeous.

It was a beautiful sunny day. The whole family met at a park where students went for prom pictures. We took photos of Kelsey with her date, her father, her grandparents, and her friends. Then we said goodbye as she left for the night.

I felt an enormous sense of relief, but I still worried. What if Kelsey had what we called "a bad pee" during the evening? We weren't in the clear until the event was over. This was an awful way to live. We never knew what to expect, and so everything was stressful. Kelsey could be fine one minute, and in extreme pain the next. Luck won out this evening, and her prom night was a success.

We weren't this fortunate for the SAT college admission test. I was asleep when I heard a strange, moaning sound. It was 2 AM. I went downstairs to find Kelsey in horrible, debilitating pain. She could hardly speak as she leaned against the back of a kitchen chair with her legs spread apart. "Bad pee," was all she said.

There wasn't much I could do but stay with her. Marty heard us and came downstairs. When Kelsey was in this much pain, she didn't like to talk. After standing this way for hours, her legs started to give out, so she switched positions. I got her a pillow so she could kneel on the tile floor and rest her head on the seat of the chair. All night long she was in either one of these positions. How could she possibly do well on the SAT after being up most of the night?

By the time Kelsey needed to leave, the pain had subsided enough for her to walk, but now she had to pee again. She decided to "hold it" until she finished taking the test. The original plan was for her to drive to the test location in her car. The new plan was for me to drop her off and pick her up when she was finished. I couldn't imagine being up half the night and taking the SAT while needing to use the bathroom. Kelsey managed to take the test under these circumstances and still get a good score.

Most students enjoy their senior year of high school. Kelsey was thinking about becoming a pediatric nurse and enrolled in a BOCES (Board of Cooperative Educational Services) program called New Visions: Health Careers. This program is designed for seniors interested in medical and health-related professions. In addition to academics, the students travel to various facilities and shadow medical professionals during their workday. To complete the program—and graduate on time—a certain number of hours are required. Again, Kelsey's burning urination interfered with her attendance. We had to keep rescheduling her hours, and soon time was running out. Kelsey wouldn't be allowed to participate in high school graduation if she didn't complete her hours. The 504 Plan allowed for extended time, but this still meant she couldn't graduate with her classmates if she didn't pass the program before the date of graduation.

The supervisor in charge of setting up the placements eventually became frustrated and stopped helping us, so I asked if I could find my own placements for Kelsey. After making call after call, I finally found a place that said yes: She would shadow a nurse who worked in a jail. At first, the nurse had her do rounds among the prisoners, but Kelsey was drawing too much attention with her looks; the prisoners were making crude comments. The nurse then decided to just keep her in the file room. Still, working at the jail gave Kelsey enough hours to graduate with her classmates. Many parents were crying at graduation as their child's name was called. When Kelsey walked across that stage and received her diploma, I felt downright giddy with happiness and utter relief.

In the meantime, all four vulvodynia specialists we consulted had recommended that Kelsey have a vestibulectomy. Since her senior year of high school had been a disaster, it was foolish to think college would be any different. We all decided that this was the best time to have the procedure. Yet again, it was terribly disappointing for her not to carry on with her life as planned. But going to college would have to wait.

In September of 2011, just two months after her high school graduation, Kelsey, Marty, and I got on a train to Manhattan. We sat in the front seat of the passenger car because there was more room to put the wheelchair we would need to get Kelsey home. The following morning, she was having a vestibulectomy. Even though it was an outpatient procedure, Dr. Gibbons explained that Kelsey should stay in the city for a few days before attempting to travel. I reserved a hotel room as close to the facility as possible.

After checking into the hotel, we wandered down the street looking for a place to eat. "What would you like for dinner?" I asked Kelsey. She was quiet, scared, and didn't want to sit in a restaurant. I grabbed some take-out burgers with fries, and we had dinner in our hotel room.

The following morning, Marty carried the wheelchair as the three of us walked to the surgical center. I couldn't imagine how Kelsey felt. Her vestibule, the area around the opening of the vagina, was about to be surgically removed. She was still quiet and scared, but walked there with confidence, believing this was something she had to do.

I was thankful when they called Kelsey's name immediately upon our arrival, so we weren't left sitting and waiting while our anxiety grew. The procedure itself didn't take long. Soon Dr. Gibbons walked into the waiting room and told us everything had gone well.

Getting Kelsey back to the hotel was difficult because of the uneven sidewalks. Even though she still had anesthetics in her system helping with pain, she winced when the wheelchair hit a bump every three or four feet. The short walk this morning now took twice as long because we were moving so slowly. Finally, we got Kelsey settled in bed at the hotel, where we stayed until she could travel. It was such a relief when a few days later we left the city by train with Kelsey in the wheelchair.

Dr. Gibbons wasn't exaggerating when he said to expect a long and painful recovery. Back home, we carried a mattress downstairs and placed it on the living room floor, since Kelsey wasn't supposed to climb stairs for several weeks. While she rested, I read comments written by women who'd had vestibulectomies. They all said that ice would be Kelsey's best friend. Every night I filled a half dozen Ziplock bags with crushed ice and placed them in a cooler. I slept on the couch next to Kelsey with the cooler on the floor between us. Several times a night, she woke up in pain, and I'd hand her a bag of ice to place between her legs. She couldn't be left alone during this recovery period. Each morning, my mom came to stay with Kelsey while I went to work.

After a few months, it was time for the follow-up appointment. Kelsey and I were incredibly anxious. Once more, she lay on the table and held my hand as Dr. Gibbons began the pelvic exam. While he was doing the Q-tip test, huge tears started pouring down her face. For a moment, my heart sank.

Kelsey saw the look on my face and realized what I was thinking. "Don't worry, Mom," she finally sobbed. "I'm crying because it doesn't hurt."

These were tears of *joy*. I couldn't believe it. When the doctor left the room, Kelsey practically leaped off the table. "It didn't hurt. It didn't hurt," she kept repeating as she got dressed.

I was euphoric. We hugged triumphantly before meeting the doctor briefly in his office. I thanked him profusely, and we left feeling like two people who had just won the lottery. Now Kelsey could go to college, get a job, and start a family. It seemed like a miracle.

Back home, there was a strange feeling in the house. Instead of being on high alert, our lives felt *normal*—possibly for the first time ever. Kelsey was happy; the worry was gone from her eyes. When she entered the bathroom, I smiled and felt grateful. Our calendar wasn't filled with medical appointments. I started to relax.

The first thing Kelsey did with her pain-free life was to get a job at a pet store. She'd come home and say, "I sold six puppy guides today. That's more than some employees sell in a week."

These booklets for new puppy owners cost twenty dollars, shared tips for how to raise a puppy, and included coupons worth over two hundred dollars. The coupons were for items a puppy owner would need, such as dog food, treats, flea and tick prevention, toys, grooming, and cleaning supplies for when the puppy inevitably peed on the floor.

"This week I sold 24 guides, the highest number in the store," Kelsey told us on a Sunday afternoon after her shift. "It's easy. When someone comes in with their puppy, I just explain the guide to them. They always say yes."

"Who knew you had a talent in sales," Marty said proudly.

Selling the most puppy guides became a big deal and got Kelsey noticed by her store manager. She was asked to share with other employees how she approached customers and was able to sell so many. There was a regional contest about which store could sell the most guides during a certain period. Kelsey sold the most in the entire region and her store won the contest because of her.

It was finally time to start college. Since Marty worked at the local community college, Kelsey decided to live at home and take classes there. She enrolled in the Fall 2012 semester and took five classes in their Graphic Arts Department. Even while working part time at the pet store, she got three A's, and A-minuses in a marketing class and a design class. Her grade point average was 3.88. I couldn't believe it. My daughter was healthy and happy and thriving in college. Our old lives of stress, fear, medical horrors, and Kelsey in pain seemed to finally be behind us.

Chapter Seven

About a year after the follow-up appointment for the vestibulectomy, Kelsey seemed to be hiding something. She kept looking at me with this sad face, and she spent more time in her bedroom than usual. "Is something wrong?" I kept asking.

"No, everything is good," she told me over and over. But I knew better. And eventually, Kelsey had no choice but to tell me. "My bottom is burning again," she said.

I shook my head, not quite understanding what she was saying. "What do you mean your bottom is burning?" I asked.

"I didn't want to tell you." She avoided looking directly at me. "At first it hurt just a little, then it hurt a little bit more. It keeps getting worse. I was hoping it would go away and get better like it was before."

The familiar dread flooded back in. How could this happen?

We went to Manhattan and saw one vulvodynia specialist after another. That damn Q-tip came out, and, once more, it hurt when pressure was put on her vulva area. Technically, she no longer had a vestibule. We were told the nerves had grown back—something I hadn't known was possible. After all we'd been through, I couldn't believe we were back to living in fear. I was reeling with the idea of starting over.

Kelsey continued taking classes and working at the pet store. The next semester she enrolled in four classes. But at night, she was awake in pain; then she'd drive to class exhausted. It was hard to do homework and study when she was tired all the time. Her teachers were told about her urinary problems, and they gave her extra time to complete assignments. That semester she got B's and her grade point average lowered to 3.08.

The following semester, I was a wreck all the time. I'd call Kelsey from work and ask, "Are you up and getting ready for class?"

"I just can't do it today," she'd say. "I've been up all night. I need to sleep."

Kelsey missed more and more classes. By mid-semester, she withdrew from a modern novel class and cardio fitness. Physical education classes were required. Exerting herself was the last thing Kelsey needed. She still managed to complete three classes, but her grades were dropping; her GPA was now 2.72. The next semester, she took only one class and withdrew after the first few weeks. Sad and sorry and deeply disappointed, we all decided that going to college was causing too much stress and pressure on the whole family.

The same thing was happening at the pet store. Even though Kelsey had reduced her hours, she was still calling in sick if she'd been up all night. If she peed at work, she often couldn't walk afterward and had to leave during her shift. If she'd had an extremely painful pee, she couldn't sit upright enough to drive home. Then she'd stay in the parking lot with the seat reclined and her feet on the dashboard until the pain subsided enough to drive safely.

The store manager was aware of these problems. She knew what a hard worker Kelsey was and still valued her as an employee. When Kelsey called in or had to leave, she was kind, supportive, and understanding. But this store manager relocated to another store and was replaced. And the new manager wasn't the least bit understanding about her medical condition. When Kelsey called in, she threatened her with termination.

One winter morning, Kelsey left for work on icy roads. My phone rang ten minutes later. Kelsey's voice was shaking, and she could barely speak. "I slid off the road and I'm in a ditch," she managed to say. "The car is on its side. I can't get out."

"Are you hurt?" I asked, as I grabbed my keys and raced out the door.

"I don't think so," Kelsey said, but she sounded unsure.

I drove to where she'd gone off the road. By the time I got there, a man had opened the passenger side door and pulled Kelsey from the car.

"My neck hurts and my legs are sore," she said. "But I'm okay."

We both started to panic, but not because of the accident. Kelsey was supposed to be at work. From the side of the road, I called the store manager and told her, "Kelsey slid on some ice and her car is in a ditch."

She responded, "The next time Kelsey doesn't show up for work, she'd better be in the hospital."

I called the corporate offices and fought for Kelsey to keep this job she loved, even though this new manager was causing her so much stress that she no longer enjoyed going to work. The corporate offices didn't care, because she didn't have proof of a disability; the 504 plan she'd had at school didn't extend to a job. Eventually, Kelsey was forced to leave this job that had once made her feel important and needed. She tried another part-time job at a convenience store, but with similar results. I understand that businesses need people they can rely on, but it was still frustrating for her to be left with no options. Now she couldn't go to college or work, which left her home, sad and isolated.

Kelsey was seeing a pelvic floor therapist who was an hour away. She'd meet me in the school parking lot, and we'd hurry to Albany. The only way I could work and take her to therapy was if we got the last appointment of the day. This type of physical therapy is recommended for women with vulvodynia. The pelvic floor is made of muscles that support the urinary tract and the reproductive tract, and they also control the bladder and bowels. When a person has pelvic floor dysfunction, these muscles aren't working together the way they should. A therapist helps women learn how to strengthen and relax their pelvic muscles. This is like biofeedback, which Kelsey had already tried, but instead of using a probe and a computer, it's with a person.

Almost all medical appointments brought us through the Albany area. Most of the time, we left these appointments feeling sad and depressed. There was a pet store at the mall that allowed people to visit with puppies that were for sale. It became a tradition for us to stop after appointments and visit the puppies, not because we wanted to buy one, but because it made us feel better. Who can be sad and depressed while a puppy is nipping at your heels, licking you, or tugging on your shoelaces?

During one of these visits, I said to Kelsey, "You pick first."

A worker brought the puppy she chose into a little white cubicle for us to play with. Then it was my turn, and I chose our second puppy. The rule was no more than three.

Kelsey said, "Mom, you pick our last puppy."

I was about to choose a Cavalier King Charles Spaniel, but at the last second, I changed my mind and said, "No, you pick."

Kelsey chose a male golden retriever. When he was brought into our cubicle, it was love at first sight. His eyes made me melt. He wasn't nipping like the other puppies his age. I took pictures of Kelsey holding him in her arms like a baby. It was difficult to give him back. He was our third puppy, so we left.

For days I couldn't stop thinking about the golden retriever. I kept looking at the pictures of him on my phone. I called the pet store. "Is the golden retriever still there?" I asked. Part of me hoped he was sold.

Only then would I be able to stop thinking about him. We already owned not one, not two, but *three* dogs!

"He's still here," the girl told me.

About a week later, Brendan and I were in the Albany area. I made up an excuse to stop at the mall because I wanted to visit the golden retriever. When we did, I still felt this overwhelming love for him. After a few days, I called the pet store. The worker knew who I was. I was the woman who kept calling about the golden retriever. She told me he was still there.

Twelve days after our first meeting, Kelsey and I drove to Albany with no intention other than seeing him again. On the car ride there, I kept telling myself, *Don't do it, Deb. Don't you dare.*

A worker brought him into our cubicle. When she came back to check on us, I said, "We're taking him home."

Kelsey was shocked and thrilled. "I knew you loved this guy, but I never thought you'd buy him!" she said.

We picked out a collar and a leash, then carried him to the car. Kelsey held him on her lap as I drove home. He kept licking her face and making us laugh. Then he fell asleep in her arms.

We named him Max, but Timmy became his nickname. This time, Cocoa and Hershey balked just a little when we brought him in— nothing like the fight they'd put up about Marley. They were much older now, and maybe less intimidated by a puppy.

Marley didn't mind at all that another dog was in the house. I'd never seen him play before, but now, he'd be lying on the floor when Max would lift a paw and swat him in the face. I didn't think this was a good idea, but after a few swats, Marley would get up and wrestle with him. They'd circle each other, pounce, and roll around. When Marley had enough, he'd just stop wrestling and go back to lying on the floor. Max would look disappointed, and then go find something else to do.

Having four large dogs probably puts me in the "bit crazed" category. But when I decided to bring Max home, aside from loving him, I did have an ulterior motive. Cocoa and Hershey were showing serious signs of old age. Their ball playing days were over. They struggled whenever they tried to lift their hips off the floor. I was already thinking, *What would I do without them?* A couple of years later, when Cocoa and Hershey died within months of each other, having Max helped me cope—just as I'd anticipated.

Kelsey continued seeing her pelvic floor therapist. Sometimes it seemed like these treatments were improving her symptoms, but it was hard to tell because her pain fluctuated. Was therapy making a difference or was it a coincidence? I wondered if repetitive, intense sessions were worth a try, versus seeing a therapist in Albany a few times a month. There is a special facility in Manhattan where people from all over the country go for pelvic floor therapy. I arranged for Kelsey to have five consecutive days of therapy in March of 2014, when Marty was on spring break. I rented a little apartment for them to stay in.

The three of us went to Manhattan on a Saturday evening. I stayed overnight with them, but the next day I hugged Kesley and said goodbye. Marty would stay with her while I went to work. It was hard for me to walk out the apartment door.

As I waited for my train, I started to cry. Even though Kelsey was now 21, I still felt the need to be present for all medical appointments. Getting on the train and going home felt like I was deserting her—but I had to go to work on Monday. Every night that week, I spoke to Marty and Kelsey on the phone about their day. They were enjoying spending time together, just the two of them. Now I was glad I'd left and given them this opportunity.

Unfortunately, though, the intense daily treatments didn't improve her symptoms.

That June, Brendan graduated from high school. We put Marty's senior picture next to Brendan's, and they looked almost identical. Brendan is 6'2"—three inches taller than Marty—but something about Brendan's build makes people think he is even taller. In September, he'd move into a dorm room at Siena College, the same school Marty went to for computer science, and start working towards a degree in electrical engineering.

I couldn't imagine the house without Brendan in it. Despite my many hours caring for Kelsey, Brendan and I had been best friends as he grew up, even when he became a teenager. Sometimes we'd go out to dinner together, just the two of us. We liked the same movies and often went to the movie theater. Animal Planet was our favorite TV station. At one point, we had water frogs in one tank, beautiful freshwater fish in another, and a third tank with two painted turtles.

In a room we called The Office was a large wire cage with two sugar gliders—small, nocturnal possums—that he'd named Bob and Bindy, because these were the names of TV "crocodile hunter" Steve Irwin's children. One morning, Brendan went downstairs and turned on the television to learn that Steve Irwin had been fatally injured by a stingray. He came upstairs to my bedroom, shook me gently awake, and said, "Mom, you're not going to believe this. Steve Irwin died!" There were tears in his eyes.

Now, he was a young man, leaving for college. On the plus side, the college he would be attending was only an hour away. We'd still get to see him whenever we wanted. It was hard for Kelsey to watch Brendan during his senior year of high school applying to different colleges and preparing to leave home, something she never got to experience.

To celebrate Brendan's graduation, we decided to go on a Caribbean cruise and invite other members of the family. I asked Kelsey, "Do you want to go? Give it some thought." Honestly, part of me was hoping she'd decide not to come. Having her on a cruise ship in the middle of the ocean sounded terrifying.

After giving it some thought, Kelsey said, "I want to go on the cruise and get to spend time with everyone. For an excursion, can I swim with the dolphins?"

Swimming with dolphins was something Kelsey had talked about since she was a little girl. We braved taking her out to what seemed like the middle of the Atlantic. The day of the excursion, she couldn't stop smiling. Kelsey, Brendan, and one of their cousins walked into an enclosure with a guide and a dozen other people. The group formed a circle. Kelsey got to touch, hold, feed, and kiss a dolphin. When the event was over, she still couldn't stop smiling. It was the most fun I'd seen her have in such a long time.

Back on the cruise ship, Kelsey peed. She got off the toilet, collapsed on the floor in her cabin, and started screaming. The saltwater had caused a serious reaction with the skin of her vulva. She cried for hours, in so much pain that she vomited. With time, her screams became more of a whimper. I felt so distraught that she could go from having the best day ever to such a horrible situation in a matter of seconds. Now, when I look at a picture of Kelsey's huge smile as she's being kissed by a dolphin, all I see is her lying on the floor and me beside her feeling helpless.

Most of Kelsey's doctors were either urologists or gynecologists. They recommended that she see a pain management specialist. Because traveling to Manhattan wasn't ideal, I thought it would be better to find someone local. The pain management office I called was less than an hour away. I asked, "When is the next available appointment?"

The woman who answered the phone said, "July 2015."

It was the first week of November. July was nine months away. If I didn't feel like crying, I might have laughed. Someone who is living in chronic pain had to wait nine months for help. "No thanks," I told her. "We'll go someplace else." I made a few more calls to other facilities and got similar answers.

My anger and frustration led me to research pain management doctors in Manhattan. The list of specialists in the city went on and on. I could get Kelsey an appointment with a highly regarded doctor within a week.

Once again, off we went to Manhattan. It didn't cause me the same amount of stress it once had, but still, travel of any kind with Kelsey made me anxious. One bad pee could put us at a standstill. But now, if there weren't parking spaces at the bus station, I would park illegally. If I got a ticket, I didn't care. Anyway, we made it again, and we easily found the pain management office on Fifth Avenue directly across from Central Park.

Kelsey and I considered ourselves experts at rating a doctor. It took us only a few moments to decide if we liked the person or not. We were waiting in these two school-like plastic chairs when a tall, dark-haired man walked into the room. He'd read the medical records I provided ahead of time, so I didn't have to summarize her life and relive the gory details.

Even though this was her first appointment, Dr. Chambers said, "I'd like to give Kelsey a pudendal nerve block today."

I couldn't believe he wasn't making us wait for prior approval from the insurance company. We wouldn't need to travel back to Manhattan for the injection. Kelsey had a regular appointment, but he was finding this extra time in his schedule.

Kelsey wasn't as happy as I was. When Dr. Chambers left the room, she said, "What is he going to do to me?" She wasn't mentally prepared for an outpatient procedure.

"This is great," I told her—easy for me to say as a bystander watching from my little plastic chair.

Before Kelsey had a chance to get more nervous, she was started on an IV, lightly sedated, and wheeled into a procedure room. Using X-ray guidance, Dr. Chambers injected her pudendal nerve, which runs through the pelvic floor muscles, with a local anesthetic and a steroid. This injection often gives immediate, temporary relief of genital, rectal, and/or tailbone pain.

After the procedure, they stopped the medication that was making Kelsey sleepy. She woke up and was told to get dressed. "I can't feel my legs," Kelsey said, as she tried to lift her feet into her pants legs. Because an anesthetic had been injected into her pudendal nerve, she was partially numb from the waist down.

I knelt on the floor, lifted Kelsey's legs for her, and then put on her shoes. With my arm around her shoulders, we shuffled our way back to Port Authority.

After a few hours, feeling slowly returned to her legs—and the first nerve block went well. For a few blessed weeks, her symptoms completely disappeared. This was a promising start. We returned six weeks later, as directed, for a second nerve block. As steroids build up in a patient's system, consecutive nerve blocks are supposed to last longer.

But the second nerve block wore off quicker than the first. This was the opposite of what was expected. We returned for a third injection, and this time Kelsey didn't have any relief. A person can only have three injections per year because of the steroids. Now we had to wait a whole year before trying again. It felt like one step forward, two steps back, over and over again.

Chapter Eight

One night I was researching vulvodynia, as I had countless times before, but something popped up that I'd never seen. It was about a gynecologist who was successfully treating vulvodynia patients by balancing their micro flora. The only problem: This doctor was in Scottsdale, Arizona.

It seemed crazy to fly to Arizona to see a doctor, but whenever I discovered something new, I always thought, maybe this is the answer. Once that thought got stuck in my head, it wouldn't go away until I followed through. Kelsey and I had driven to see doctors in many places, but we'd never flown anywhere for an appointment. In March of 2015, we got on a plane in Newark and landed in Phoenix, Arizona.

I couldn't stop staring out the window of the rental car as we drove from Phoenix to our hotel in Scottsdale. "This doesn't look anything like I imagined," I said. Instead of a flat, brown landscape, like the deserts I'd seen on television, there were mountains, rock formations, and gorgeous plant life everywhere.

Kelsey agreed. "I didn't know a desert could be so beautiful," she said.

We pulled up to an impressive looking hotel. I had seen photos of it online when I'd reserved our standard room for two nights, but it looked much fancier in person, with huge white columns surrounding a circular drive. There were flowering plants with bright colors: pink, lavender, yellow.

Kelsey and I walked through the lobby to the check-in desk. I told the man behind the counter my name. When he looked up our reservation on the computer, he said, "Today is your lucky day. We overbooked our standard rooms, and you were chosen to get a villa."

Alarms went off in my head that told me I was about to be conned. I said, "You mean you're giving us a villa, but only charging me for a standard room."

He said, "Yes."

I still didn't believe him. I repeated myself in a slightly different way, "I'm not going to be charged any more money than if we stayed in a standard room?"

The man laughed, finding my questions amusing. "I promise," he assured me. "You're only going to be charged for a standard room." Then he handed me a map.

As we walked away from the desk, Kelsey took the map from my hand. "What's a villa?" she asked.

"I'm not sure, but it sounds much better than a hotel room," I said.

The map was necessary because the hotel grounds were like a village, with everything you could possibly want or need. As we located the villas, we went by hotel buildings, a restaurant, a main pool area, smaller pools, several hot tubs, a gym, and a spa—all with beautiful, impressive landscaping, as if we were in a dreamy neighborhood. I hadn't seen the villa yet and I already wanted to live here. There were street signs that helped guide us to the address of our place. When we arrived, it looked like a little house with its own walkway and front door.

I parked the car and took out our luggage. We couldn't wait to discover what was behind that door. When Kelsey opened it, there was a full-size living room with couches, chairs, a television, and a table. The living room had a door that led to a large bedroom with two queen-size beds. Outside the bathroom were double sinks and mirrors.

"I can't believe we get to stay here," Kelsey kept saying as we walked around.

We opened a sliding glass door to find a backyard with our own furnished patio. The appointment wasn't until tomorrow morning. Instead of taking the time to unpack, we put on our swimsuits and hurried to one of the pools.

When we got back to the villa, Kelsey put on a plush, white robe she found hanging in the closet for guests. We sat outside on our private patio. With her feet resting on a chair and sunglasses shielding her eyes, she said, "Take my picture. I feel rich and famous."

*　　*　　*

The following morning, we met Dr. Fraser. It was a brief appointment, considering we'd flown all the way to Arizona. His specialized test only required a swab and then waiting for the results. He said he'd contact us in a week and make recommendations based on what the testing showed.

I called Marty after the appointment. "Arizona is gorgeous," I told him. "I'm looking online at houses for sale. Today is going to be sunny and 85."

"Enjoy it while you can," Marty reminded me. "The temperature here is 34. It's overcast and gloomy."

Kelsey and I had the whole day ahead of us. Women with vulvodynia aren't supposed to go horseback riding, but we figured this one time would be okay. I made a late afternoon reservation for us to go on a trail ride. In the meantime, we had lunch in downtown Scottsdale and walked around the shops. When it was time, we drove away from civilization to find the horseback riding facility.

As we walked around the old wooden buildings looking for an employee, it felt like we were on the movie set for an upcoming western. The horses were standing in a shaded outdoor stable without walls. Because we'd been shopping in Scottsdale, we arrived wearing shorts, T-shirts, and sandals. Among the old buildings, we found a bathroom, where we changed into jeans and appropriate footwear. I was beginning to worry that maybe we were in the wrong place when a man appeared.

"You must be here for the trail ride," he said. "It's just the two of you. We'll saddle up the horses and leave in ten minutes."

When the time came, Kelsey and I mounted our horses, both chestnut colored with a white blaze down their faces. As we rode through the Sonoran Desert, it felt surreal that I was with Kelsey in Arizona on horses enjoying this incredible experience. For so many years, so much of our time together had been filled with her discomfort or pain; this felt like a gorgeous, unexpected reprieve. The plant life and scenery were different from anything we'd ever seen before: tall saguaro cacti, barrel cacti, pops of different colored flowers. We were swooning at every new plant, every beautiful view of the mountains in the background. Exactly as we reached the end of the trail, the sun began to set, and the sky turned different shades of pink and purple.

It was dinnertime when we drove back to Scottsdale. Kelsey wanted to eat at an Italian restaurant she'd noticed when we were walking around earlier. As we got closer to the restaurant, I could see a huge line of people waiting to get in. I was about to tell Kelsey we needed to find someplace else to eat, but then I decided it wouldn't hurt to ask.

"We need a table for two. How long would the wait be?" I asked the woman standing outside at a reservation desk.

She said, "Follow me."

As she led us to a table, Kelsey and I gave each other questioning looks. Why had she given us a table while all those people were waiting in line? I'll admit I didn't feel guilty, though—just grateful. The Italian dishes we ordered were delicious.

The owner of the restaurant approached our table as we were finishing. "I hope you enjoyed your meals," he said. "Do you live around here?"

"We're from Upstate New York," I told him. "My daughter had a medical appointment this morning. Our meals were wonderful."

He called over our waitress and said, "Dessert's on the house."

It was late when we got back to the villa, but I wanted to enjoy a dip in the hot tub. Kelsey sat in a chair next to me. While we were sitting there, a fireworks show started. We wondered why there were fireworks in the middle of March. Then I decided. "The fireworks are for us," I told Kelsey. "These have been the luckiest two days of our lives. We should go buy a lottery ticket."

Our flight wasn't until 11:00 the following evening. This meant we got to spend one more day lounging by the pool, enjoying a dip in the hot tub, and then going for a swim. When it was time to leave for the airport, we said goodbye to paradise.

As soon as we landed in Newark, Kelsey had a bad pee. She came out of the bathroom and said, "Can you find me some ice?"

I went to a fast-food counter. Because I can't tell people why I really need ice, I said to the worker, "Could I have a small bag of ice for an injury?"

The girl behind the counter said, "We're not allowed to give out ice."

I turned to Kelsey, "I guess we're home," I said, thinking of the wonderful people we'd met in Arizona. Then I went in search of a kinder person who wasn't possessive of their ice.

As it turned out, Dr. Fraser didn't resolve Kelsey's pain, but he did recommend an anti-inflammatory rinse which she used for many years. Even though the trip wasn't a medical success, we were thankful for the wonderful memories. It felt like someone had taken mercy on us for three days and made everything perfect. I always referred to this trip as magical.

Chapter Nine

When the second series of pudendal nerve blocks didn't give Kelsey relief, Dr. Chambers recommended a spinal cord stimulator (SCS). When a person feels pain, it is because certain nerves are sending pain signals to their brain. The stimulator has a pulse generator with thin wires called leads that get implanted during a surgical procedure. Tiny pulses of electric current go through the leads to nerves on the spinal cord. The pulses mask pain signals traveling to the brain.

Before considering another surgery, I made appointments for Kelsey in the gynecology and urology departments of Cleveland Clinic in Ohio. I thought if things went well, we'd come back and see doctors in other departments. It was always my goal to find one medical facility to manage all her care. At the time, their urology department was rated number two in the country, with Mayo Clinic in Minnesota ranked number one. Maybe the doctors at Cleveland Clinic would have suggestions we hadn't tried yet. We left Canajoharie and drove for six hours until we arrived at our hotel for a one-night stay.

The following morning, we pulled onto the Cleveland Clinic campus. I wonder if doctors realize that what they say to a patient might always stay with them. First, we saw a gynecologist. He looked at Kelsey's history and said, "I can't wave a magic wand over you and make you better." Next, we went to the urology department. The urologist looked at her medical records and said, "You've already been to the best, why did you come here?"

I didn't say it out loud, but I was thinking, I came here because I thought *you* were the best. After driving six hours, his question was harsh and almost made me cry right there in the office. But crying could wait. I explained to him that the pain management specialist was recommending a spinal cord stimulator. The urologist agreed and thought Kelsey should try one.

Once we were in the parking lot, there was no need to hide the tears. I gave Kelsey a hug and we both cried before getting in the car. We felt defeated as we began the long drive home. I was usually eager to meet new doctors, and often left feeling hopeless. Sometimes neither of us had the energy to keep fighting.

And now we were considering another surgery.

The first step was to do a trial for a spinal cord stimulator. This is like test driving a car before buying it. The patient wears a temporary system externally for several days, and then the system is easily removed. Based on the results of the trial, the patient decides if they want the surgery.

Dr. Chambers did this procedure only in his Staten Island location, which we had never been to before. Kelsey was nervous as I drove the three and a half hours to get there. "It sounds painful to have wires coming out of my back," she said.

I certainly agreed, but always tried to make things seem like they weren't a big deal. "It's only for five days," I reminded her. "And if it helps with your pain, it will be worth it."

While Kelsey was sedated, Dr. Chambers put temporary leads in her back that came out through her skin and were taped down along with an external stimulator. Each day she wore the system, Kelsey said, "I'm not having pain." The trial was a huge success. After the failed vestibulectomy, we were cautiously optimistic.

We drove to Staten Island so Dr. Chambers could remove the external system. "I had a great week," Kelsey told him. "It didn't burn when I peed." This was an option worth pursuing, but at that moment, she was scared to have another surgery. When we left the office, she said, "I want to think about it."

On our drive home, Kelsey asked me to stop because she needed to pee. This would be the first time she urinated since having the trial system removed. I pulled over at a gas station.

A few minutes later, Kelsey came running out of the bathroom. I was sitting in the driver's seat and put the passenger window down because I didn't know why she was running. As she got closer, I could tell she was screaming.

She leaned into the window, gasping for air. "Find me some ice," she begged. "I need to have the surgery." The difference between wearing the trial system and then having it removed was so drastic that she immediately overcame her fears.

Dr. Chambers referred us to a neurosurgeon who would implant a permanent spinal cord stimulator. Of course, he too was in Manhattan. We met Dr. Manning for a consultation. He said, "I'll put a metal plate on Kelsey's spine with leads that should block her pain signals. This device will prevent her from being able to have MRIs in the future."

A clipboard filled with papers was put in front of Kelsey to sign. I figured a pain-free life was worth the sacrifice of no MRIs. We left the consultation with a surgical date in September of 2015—only one month away, since they'd had a cancellation.

The night before the surgery, Kelsey and I stayed in a hotel near the hospital. In the morning, we took a taxi. I couldn't believe the number of surgical patients in the waiting room. This was a huge hospital. Eventually a nurse opened the door and said, "Kelsey Waffle."

We both stood up and walked toward the door. The nurse stopped me. "I'm sorry," she explained. "Only patients are allowed beyond this point."

In other facilities, I'd always been with Kelsey when an IV was started, questions were asked, and the surgeon and anesthesiologist stopped by. Not here. Kelsey looked back at me with terror in her eyes.

"You'll be fine," I assured her. "I'll be right here waiting, and I'll see you in recovery."

She hugged me, still looking scared as she followed the nurse through the door.

Implanting a permanent SCS was much more complicated than the trial. A metal plate would be attached to her spine. Leads were being routed to a battery implanted on the left side of her buttock. The plate required a five-inch incision, and then there'd be another incision for the battery.

The number of monitors in the waiting room made it feel like an airport. I was given a six-digit number to track Kelsey's progress—pre-surgery, surgery, and recovery. Reading a book helped distract me from staring at the screens. I only allowed myself to check on her progress every fifteen minutes.

Finally, the screen changed from surgery to recovery. A nurse called my name and let me sit with Kelsey while she was waking up. Then I followed as Kelsey was taken to a hospital room for a one-night stay. She pressed her call button to use the bathroom, but no one came, so she pressed it again.

When a nurse finally showed up, she told me, "I have a bad back, you're going to need to get her out of bed."

The nurse gave me directions on how to get Kelsey upright, turn her legs to the side so she was seated, and then lift her to a standing position. After a few hours, I knew I couldn't leave Kelsey here alone overnight.

I said, "I'll be right back." It was already dark when I got in the taxi. I got our belongings from the hotel, canceled my reservation, and hurried back to the hospital.

The following day, the process was started for Kelsey to be discharged. A nurse was giving us directions and paperwork to sign. When I looked at Kelsey, I noticed her cheeks were flushed and her eyes were glossy. "I think she has a fever," I said. "Would you take her temperature?"

The nurse responded, "No, she's already set to be discharged. Her temperature was taken a couple of hours ago and it was normal."

I couldn't believe I was in a hospital and a nurse was refusing to take a patient's temperature. Instead of arguing, I waited for her to leave, and then walked to the main desk where there were many other nurses. The woman that refused my request wasn't there.

"I think my daughter has a fever," I told a nurse. "Would someone take her temperature?"

One of the nurses said, "Sure, I'll be right there." Within minutes, she arrived and clocked Kelsey's temperature between 101 and 102. "Well," she said to Kelsey, "I guess you're not going home today."

The discharge was put on hold. Later, the original nurse came into the room, furious that I had disobeyed her. I couldn't imagine why it mattered to this nurse whether a patient stayed an extra day or not.

The following morning Kelsey's temperature was normal, and she was discharged. During the three-hour drive home, every little bump on the thruway caused her pain. It was a relief to pull into our driveway after being away for several days. Marty had already put a mattress on the living room floor so Kelsey wouldn't have to climb the stairs. Once again, she endured a painful recovery as the incisions on her back slowly healed.

*   *   *

About six weeks after the surgery, we went to Dr. Chambers's office to meet Leah, a representative from the SCS company. She shared her story with us. "I was on a sidewalk in Manhattan when a driver exiting a parking garage ran over me. The pain in my back made it impossible for me to do anything. I thought I'd have to live with that debilitating pain for the rest of my life. Then I got a spinal cord stimulator. Now I'm married and pregnant with my first child."

Her story was inspiring. I imagined the SCS giving Kelsey back her life, just as it had for Leah. She used a computer to connect with Kelsey's internal system. Then she designed various programs. Some were silent, which meant Kelsey wouldn't feel anything. Others made a tingly or pulse-like sensation. Each program was named and displayed on a handheld remote. Leah called one "Bubbles" because she said it reminded her of champagne. Kelsey was encouraged to experiment and see which programs she liked. We left feeling hopeful.

For the next few days, every time Kelsey came out of the bathroom, I bombarded her with questions, "How do you feel? Did it burn? Does it hurt?"

"It doesn't hurt that bad," she'd tell me, or, "It only burned a little."

Then I'd interrogate her further, "What do you mean it only burned a little?" I was anxious to know if the SCS was working. We were told that it might take a while for the programs to take effect, so I tried not to panic, but I could tell Kelsey wasn't being honest because she didn't want to upset me.

About a week after the programming, Kelsey finally confessed, "My bottom is still burning!"

The system should have been working by then. We were confused and upset, since the trial had been successful. When I explained this to Dr. Chambers, he said, "During the trial, I put the leads much lower on her spine."

I spoke to the surgeon and asked questions about the lead placement. He said, "The spine is like a stream. Leads placed higher up the stream should still work."

I took Kelsey to see two local pain management specialists, Dr. Kent and Dr. Andrews. On purpose, I didn't give them any background information. When they X-rayed the system in Kelsey's back, they both said the same thing. "No wonder she isn't getting relief. The leads have migrated."

Migrated meant the leads had moved and were no longer where they were supposed to be. Only then did I say, "The leads are exactly where the surgeon placed them."

"It's a shame he used that metal plate," said Dr. Kent. "If he hadn't, I could use spaghetti leads and replicate the successful trial."

Dr. Andrews said, "He may as well have put the leads in New Jersey."

We kept going back to Manhattan for reprogramming. During each visit, Leah or another representative from the company created new programs for Kelsey to try. No matter how many times the device was reprogrammed, it didn't give Kelsey relief from her painful symptoms. Eventually we turned the system off, but it stayed in her back. There was no easy way to remove the metal plate from her spine.

By the time Kelsey had this surgery, we had been traveling into the city for six years—since we'd first met the vulvodynia specialist in 2009. I had learned—we both had—how to problem solve and become self-sufficient, how to get around and what to bring. The night before any appointment in the city, I'd fill my backpack with a couple of phone chargers, drinks, snacks, sweatshirts, and possibly hats and gloves, depending on the time of year. I called it the Manhattan Survival Kit. Kelsey usually needed to pee during our trips, which could easily take more than twelve hours, and I couldn't always find ice. Now I brought a small cooler filled with frozen water bottles. I would hand her the ice before she entered the bathroom so she could apply the soothing treatment immediately.

A few times Marty took Kelsey to the pain management office to see Dr. Chambers. The night before one appointment, I held up my empty backpack and asked, "Would you like me to put together the Manhattan Survival Kit?"

He said, "No thanks. We'll be fine."

The next morning, they headed to Manhattan, and I went to work. My phone rang about 2:00. "They put Kelsey on an IV and then something went wrong with Dr. Chambers's schedule," Marty explained. "We've been waiting for hours, and I can't leave because the doctor could stop by at any moment. I haven't had anything to eat or drink all day. Now I have a killer headache."

Marty was having an awful day. I felt bad, yet couldn't resist teasing him when I said, "Maybe you shouldn't have declined the Manhattan Survival Kit."

By then, Kelsey was just plain tired of all of it. I had dragged her around the city for years, and no one was making her feel better. She'd lost faith in all medical professionals. Still, a part of me couldn't give up. To save time, occasionally I'd make two appointments on the same day.

On one trip, I made a hotel reservation because the two appointments were on consecutive days. The first appointment was futile; we got no cures and no new information. "Let's just go home," Kelsey said as we left the office. "I'm tired and I don't want to do this again tomorrow. What's the point?"

"We already have an appointment with a urologist and a paid hotel room," I told her. "Let's just make the best of it."

Kelsey was even more annoyed the next day. The appointment was early in the morning, and she fell asleep in the waiting room. I had to wake her when the nurse called her name. She followed me down the hall with heavy steps, still groggy.

The doctor must have noticed her negative body language and the angry stare she gave me as we sat across from him. "So, Kelsey, what problems are you having other than your mother?" Dr. Kendall asked.

I laughed. I thought this was the funniest thing any doctor had ever said, and we were meeting him for the first time. I immediately liked him. Later, when Kelsey was less tired, she thought this was funny too.

We saw Dr. Kendall several more times. As Kelsey could have predicted, he didn't help with her symptoms, but for years I'd occasionally turn to her and say, "So Kelsey, what problems are you having other than your mother?"

Chapter Ten

When Kelsey was 22, she developed a new symptom. She'd have a full bladder and the urge to urinate, but when she sat on the toilet, she couldn't start a stream of urine. Nothing came out, no matter how hard she tried. She could go more than 24 hours being unable to pee. The pain and pressure in her bladder would become unbearable. When she finally got the pee out, her urethra would be on fire.

Dr. Evans, a urologist in Albany, wanted to do a urodynamic study. Kelsey was terrified to have this test because it required a tube being pushed up her urethra. The doctor said she'd use a pediatric tube, which would be smaller in diameter and therefore less painful. Eventually, Kelsey agreed. During the test, Kelsey's bladder was filled with liquid while images were taken of her bladder and kidneys. Then more images were taken as she urinated. Kelsey tolerated the test better than we anticipated.

The study showed that Kelsey had a primary bladder neck obstruction and dysfunctional voiding. The bladder neck is a group of muscles that connect the bladder to the urethra. To release urine, these muscles need to relax. Dr. Evans explained that her bladder neck wasn't opening properly, which was the reason for her difficulty. She wanted to dilate Kelsey's bladder neck, which meant inserting tubes that gradually got wider through her urethra.

Whenever Kelsey had a procedure, she always refused a catheter, because it irritated her urethra and gave her more pain. Now, she said, "There is no way I'm having my urethra dilated!" Dilation sounded ten times worse than having a catheter. I couldn't blame her.

Then, on Memorial Day weekend of 2016—just nine months after having the SCS surgery—Kelsey had a debilitating pee. Her bladder had been burning for the last few days, which was also a new symptom. When several hours went by and the pain wasn't improving, Marty and I took her to the emergency room. I'm not sure why this time they admitted her to the hospital, something they had never done before. Maybe it was because she had recently seen Dr. Evans, who was associated with the hospital.

At first, they put Kelsey in the gynecology department, where women were in labor and delivering babies. After a couple of days, the nurses thought this wasn't the right placement for her and sent us to a different part of the hospital.

The hospital had six different buildings, A through F, all connected with hallways. Dr. Evans met us in Kelsey's hospital room. "I'd like to insert a tube into Kelsey's bladder," she explained. "Then urine would drain through the tube into a bag attached to her leg. While she's sedated, I think I should use dilators to widen her bladder neck since it isn't opening properly. Maybe if Kelsey didn't have to pee through her urethra, she could live a normal life."

When Dr. Evans left the room, all I retained was, "Maybe Kelsey could live a normal life."

But Kelsey said, "There's no way I'm wearing a urine bag."

"It's worth a try," I suggested.

Marty and I convinced Kelsey to have the procedure. If permanently wearing a urine bag eliminated her pain, it would be worth it. I think she agreed only because she thought it would make us happy. Dr. Evans made everything sound like it wasn't a big deal. If the procedure didn't work, all she had to do was remove the tube and Kelsey would go back to peeing through her urethra.

A surgical date was set for Kelsey to have the dilation and a tube placed in her bladder. Dr. Evans had said it made sense to dilate her bladder neck while she was already under anesthesia. One morning they took Kelsey away while Marty and I waited in her hospital room. I prayed this decision would end her chronic pain. It made sense that if urine didn't pass through her urethra, the burning would stop.

When Kelsey was brought back to the room, her whole body was shaking. It looked like she was having a seizure. The tube inserted into her bladder was causing severe bladder spasms. She'd never experienced this before and didn't understand what was happening.

"Sometimes the bladder reacts negatively to the tube, thinking it's a foreign object," Dr. Evans explained. "With time, her bladder will get used to the tube. Meanwhile, we'll give Kelsey medications to control the spasms."

Dr. Evans was wrong; none of the medications prevented the spasms in her bladder. Each morning, the medical team stopped by during rounds to evaluate the situation. They wanted Kelsey to have an infusion of Ketamine, an anesthetic that can be used for post-operative and chronic pain. Because of possible side effects, the infusion is given in Step-down ICU where patients can be closely monitored. I didn't know this at the time, but with a Ketamine infusion, you're only allowed to stay in Step-down ICU for 24 hours.

When our 24 hours were up, Kelsey was being sent to E216. A woman was wheeling Kelsey on her bed down the hall. She leaned over and whispered to me, "Don't stay there."

Confused, I whispered back, "What do you mean?"

She repeated, "Do not let your daughter stay in this part of the hospital."

"Then where do we want to go?" I asked.

"B6," she said.

As we got closer to E216, I started to understand her warning. We passed by a door with massive security measures. A sign next to it said no patient was allowed to enter or leave without supervision. I wondered if the patients behind that door were considered dangerous. This was an old part of the hospital. There weren't any windows, so the lack of natural light made the dark hallway look scary.

Kelsey had heard what the woman said. Lying down flat made it difficult for her to see. She started turning her head to the left and right to get a better view of her surroundings. The woman dropped us off in a large room with four other patients in beds lined up against the back wall.

As soon as she left, Kelsey said, "I don't want to stay here."

I was also concerned but trying to stay positive. "Let's give it a chance," I suggested. "The four walls don't matter if the nurses take good care of you."

The first thing we noticed was how hot the room felt, the burning type of heat like you'd feel in a sauna. It was June. I put my hand over a vent and heat was pouring out instead of cool air. Someone already must have complained, because a man came in to fix it. I watched him open the unit and adjust a knob using medical instruments instead of tools.

Kelsey was on a pain pump that started making a loud, repetitive beeping sound. I called in a nurse because I didn't know what this meant. She couldn't figure out why the pump was beeping, so she stepped into the hall and called in another nurse. He couldn't figure it out either and they called in a third nurse. The three of them were staring at the pump looking confused. Then they started randomly pressing buttons. I heard one of them say, "Let's just override it."

I had no idea what that meant but overriding it didn't sound like a good plan when they didn't know why it was beeping. "Step away from the pump," I told them before leaving the room and walking to the nurse's station. The woman who had warned us not to stay here was obviously right. I had just told Kelsey the four walls didn't matter. Now, I said to the nurse at the desk, "We're not staying here."

"You have to," she told me. "Where you stay is not a choice."

"The nurses don't know how to work the pain pump. We are moving." She argued with me for a while, and then I said, "If you won't move us, I'll find someone who will." I remembered what the woman had whispered to me. "We want to go to B6," I added.

The nurse looked at the computer and said, "There aren't any beds on B6, but there's one on C5."

"Then please move us to C5." I had no idea what C5 would be like, but I took my chances it would be better than here.

The nurse who agreed to move us seemed to be in charge. She got the pump to stop beeping while I gathered up our belongings. Marty had walked down the street to get a list of things from CVS. Just as Kelsey was being wheeled out of E216, he came down the hall.

"What's going on?" he asked. I explained to him what had transpired during his brief absence.

Kelsey was wheeled to C524. The nurse assigned to this room introduced herself and spent time talking to us. We immediately felt she was friendly and competent. I didn't even have time to unpack our belongings when Kelsey started crying because of a bladder spasm.

A man came into the room and said, "We're moving you to D518."

"Why?" I asked. "We just got here." I really didn't want to leave this competent nurse and risk ending up in another awful place.

"We need that bed," he explained, pointing to the empty bed next to Kelsey. "Her crying will disturb the other patient. We're going to find her a private room."

A private room did sound appealing, especially since it wasn't just Kelsey but all three of us. Still, I felt annoyed and exhausted. It was the middle of the night. In less than two hours, we were moving for the third time; from Step-down ICU to the horrible place, to this better place, and now to another unknown location.

While Kelsey was being wheeled to D518, we saw a short broad man in a hospital gown with a headful of dark, curly hair that flew in all directions. He was mostly staring at the floor, but then he'd look up to see where he was before putting his head back down. This description isn't why he drew our attention; it was the two guards walking on each side of him.

One of the guards said, "Don't even think about it, Louie."

Just as the guard said this, Louie turned and ran, bumping into a random person and almost knocking the man to the floor. Next Louie darted into a room. The guards grabbed him, and then the three of them continued their walk. Even though this man had guards, I was shocked that he was allowed to roam the halls.

The original plan was for Kelsey to have the urine bag put in place and then go home. But now, because they couldn't control the bladder spasms even with IV medications, we were trapped in the hospital. Marty and I never left Kelsey alone. I slept in a reclining chair while Marty slept on the floor with a roll-pad he used for motorcycle trips.

A nurse walked into our room one day, looked directly at me, and said, "You know there are two showers for visitors in building C on the seventh floor."

I did not know this. If our hospital room had a shower, it was for patients only, and this rule was enforced. I appreciated her sharing this information, but I also thought, *Wow, I must look awful.* I put together a backpack of everything I needed to shower regularly. It was such a treat to take a hot shower every day. As needed, Marty made the hour drive home to do laundry and bring back clean clothes.

Kelsey was having bladder spasms several times a day. The moment one started, I'd push the call button for the nurse, who then put in a request for the doctor. At night, it usually took two or three hours, sometimes longer, for a doctor to show up. The whole time we waited, Kelsey would be screaming in pain while her entire body shook uncontrollably. The doctor then ordered additional medication to go in the IV line. Once Kelsey was given this medication, the spasm would lessen within minutes and the pain would subside.

It was infuriating that Kelsey was being left to suffer when there was such a simple and immediate solution. "Why can't this medication be prescribed by the doctor, put in Kelsey's chart, and given as needed?" I asked one of the nurses.

"It doesn't work that way," the nurse explained. "This is a controlled substance, and a new script needs to be written every time."

I was still confused. "But why does it take so long for a doctor to get here?"

The nurse said, "At night, there is only one doctor for the entire hospital."

I didn't believe her. The next time we waited for a doctor, I asked him. He said, "That's right. I'm the only doctor here tonight."

Shortly after this discovery, Kelsey had a bladder spasm that started around midnight. I hit the call button and then the nightmare began. Would the doctor arrive in fifteen minutes, one hour, maybe three? We never knew the answer to this question. With each minute that passed, our anxiety grew.

After listening to Kelsey scream for almost four hours, Marty stormed out of the room looking like he was going to explode. I hurried after him, thinking I needed to diffuse whatever was about to happen.

Marty approached the central desk where all the nurses were. He reached his hand under the protective plexiglass, pounded his fist on the counter, and shouted, "Where's the doctor?"

"Get a fucking doctor here now!" I echoed. As these words left my mouth, I looked around as if someone else had said them. Nope, just me. Instead of diffusing the situation, I was a participant, making things even worse. But for so long, our daughter had been suffering, and we along with her, listening to her cries for help. We had reached our breaking point. Anyone would, it seems to me.

The nurse called security. I worried that we were about to get thrown out of the hospital, leaving Kelsey alone to fend for herself.

Two security guards came walking down the hall. One of the guards said, "Is that your daughter crying?" He could hear Kelsey from where we stood.

"Yes," Marty answered, his hands still shaking. "And we've been waiting hours for a doctor."

The guard said, "If that were my daughter, I'd be upset too." Then he stepped aside with Marty, leaving me alone with the other guard.

"You know there's a patient advocate team," my guard explained. "If you tell the nurse you're calling a 914, the team has to be called, and they're required to come right away."

The guard with Marty came back. He said, "We understand your frustration, but you need to stay calm and in control of yourselves." Then the guards left us with this reminder.

We went back to Kelsey's room. I told Marty what the security guard said, feeling like I'd been given a secret code. The guard had made this team sound like superheroes who would magically appear in the night and solve all our problems. I doubted what he said. The only way to find out was to give it a try.

The next time Kelsey had a bladder spasm at night, I hit the call button. At first, we waited. I kept looking down the hall, but there was no doctor in sight. After waiting what I considered a reasonable amount of time, I hit the call button again. This time, when the nurse walked in, I said, "I'm calling a 914."

She looked annoyed, but within minutes the patient advocate team was at the door, giving Kelsey the medication that stopped her bladder spasms. I couldn't believe it! Had this really been available all along? Now we had some control when put in this terrible situation, a way to get Kelsey relief. We called for the patient advocate team several times during our extended stay.

*   *   *

Patients who are in the hospital for long periods of time are encouraged to go on short walks as much as possible. It seemed like whenever we left our room, no matter which direction we went, there was Louie with his two guards. Nothing against Louie, but Kelsey was terrified of him. She had seen him charge into a man like a raging bull. If Louie charged into Kelsey, she'd get hurt.

To protect her, Marty always walked beside Kelsey and rolled the IV pole. It was my job to watch out for Louie. I stayed a little ahead of them so I could peek around corners and walked backwards to see who was coming from behind.

Marty and Kelsey knew what to do if I said, "Unicorn, unicorn."

This was a silly code word that meant Louie had been spotted. Then Marty would steer Kelsey from the center hallway, and she'd press herself against the wall. As he passed, we both stood in front of her in case Louie decided to bolt.

Marty and I considered it a treat to leave the hospital room for any reason; a change of scenery and fresh air were something we craved. Marty would say, "I'll go to the cafeteria. What do you guys want for breakfast?" I'd be envious because he got to leave instead of me. Even though the hospital provided meals for Kelsey, the food for patients was terrible. The food in the cafeteria, in contrast, was actually very good.

Most mornings, Kelsey and I said, "Pancakes and bacon." That was our favorite meal. We joked that when we got out, we'd come back just to have breakfast. Marty's favorite day of the week was Turkey Tuesday. On that day, the cafeteria made fresh turkey sandwiches for lunch.

When you live in a hospital, you become a hoarder. You begin to think that everything you come across might come in handy. If someone walked to the CVS, we saved the plastic bag. We ended up with a huge collection of them that traveled with us every time we moved. If I came across a tiny bottle of shampoo, I put it in my backpack. You never knew when someone might need more pancake syrup. We accumulated sticky notes, pens, and ketchup packets.

One night Marty was eating a sandwich in the hospital room. He said, "Have you seen the barbecue sauce?"

I said, "Oh yeah, the barbecue sauce is in the shower." After I said this, I burst out laughing. This is a sentence you never imagine yourself saying. Our entire time in the hospital was horrible, but we did our best to keep Kelsey's spirits up by finding humor whenever we had the opportunity.

One morning, a doctor we hadn't met came in to talk to us, as often happened. He casually mentioned that the tube in Kelsey's bladder would need to be replaced every 6 to 8 weeks for the rest of her life. Otherwise, it would get infected. How had no one explained this to us before? We had thought the tube just stayed there the whole time Kelsey wore the urine bag. This new information sent me to a new level of panic. It stood to reason that when they changed the tube, it would irritate her bladder, and the bladder spasms would just keep happening indefinitely. She had already been here now for several weeks, and they showed little sign of abating.

Before I had time to track down the urologist and ask questions, they decided to give Kelsey another infusion of Ketamine. This meant gathering up our belongings and moving to Step-down ICU again. Now I knew that in 24 hours we'd be sent to an unknown location. I told the nurse in charge, "When our time is up, please don't send us to E2." That was the awful place where the nurses hadn't known how to work the pain pump.

She said, "Where do you want to go?"

I couldn't believe someone was asking me this question. I remembered the woman who whispered to me, "You want to go to B6." I had no idea what that meant, but I said, "We'd like to go to B6."

The nurse went on the computer and said, "There's one room available, but if you want it, you need to leave immediately."

I said, "We'll take it."

Within minutes, I packed up all our things and practically ran from Step-down ICU. The nurse made it sound like someone might beat us there, and whoever got there first won. I trusted this stranger who told me I wanted to go to B6 without knowing why. Once we arrived, I had the answer. Everything was brand new. The room was enormous compared to the previous rooms we'd stayed in. There was a large couch for me to sleep on instead of a chair. The bathroom alone was the size of some hospital rooms. Now when people visited Kelsey, it felt like we were in a living room. We started calling it the hotel.

With time, the bladder spasms became bearable and less frequent. Kelsey was discharged wearing the urine bag. We left hoping this was the answer.

Chapter Eleven

We were home for 24 days. I was terrified to let anyone touch that tube, but they said it had to be changed or Kelsey was at risk of serious infection. Because things had gone so poorly, Dr. Evans wanted to remove the tube and have Kelsey try to urinate through her urethra. They called this a voiding trial.

While she was sedated, they removed the tube from her bladder. Kelsey woke up without the urine bag. We were left to wait until she felt the urge to pee. When her bladder was full and she pushed the urine through her urethra, she cried, "It feels like I'm peeing sharp pieces of glass." The voiding trial had failed miserably.

Dr. Evans concluded that Kelsey's urethra needed more time to heal from the dilation, and she surgically put a new tube in her bladder on the same day. Just as I suspected, this restarted the bladder spasms, and once again we became permanent residents of the hospital. We concluded that listening to the doctor had been a huge mistake. I felt responsible because I had convinced Kelsey to do this.

That summer we spent a total of 49 days in the hospital and slept in 10 different locations. When we finally left, the urine bag and tube were permanently removed. All this time Kelsey had suffered for no reason.

Dr. Evans thought maybe something was wrong with Kelsey's nervous system. She wanted her to see a neurologist and be tested for something called small fiber neuropathy (SFN). We had never heard of this condition before. When I first read about small fiber neuropathy, the description didn't at all fit Kelsey. The presenting symptom in three-fourths of SFN patients was pain or burning in the feet. It was usually associated with diabetes, and the average age of diagnosis was 54. Kelsey was 23, didn't have diabetes, and had never had pain in her feet.

"This won't hurt a bit," Dr. Adams told Kelsey as he put a numbing agent on the back of her calf and thigh. Then he used a small metal instrument to remove a 3mm diameter piece of skin from both places. "I'll call with the results." As promised, it didn't hurt, and Kelsey left with two band-aids.

Dr. Adams called a couple of weeks later and said, "Kelsey's biopsy for small fiber neuropathy was positive." During this type of biopsy, the density, or number of small nerve fibers, are counted. Finding an abnormally low density means the small nerve fibers are so damaged that they no longer exist.

My original understanding of SFN was very limited. Even neurologists find it difficult to explain the complexity of this condition and its possible repercussions for patients. The peripheral nervous system is made up of nerves that branch off from the spinal cord to all other parts of the body. If you were to take a cross section of a peripheral nerve, you would find it lined with small nerve fibers. With SFN, these nerve fibers have become damaged.

A key job of small nerve fibers is to sense pain. These fibers in the skin carry information about pain, temperature, and other sensations to the brain. Many patients with SFN have stabbing pain, intense burning, numbness, and/or tingling in their feet, arms, or trunk. Diabetes is the most common cause, and doctors will categorize these patients as having diabetic neuropathy. Because most patients have more than one type of nerve fiber involved, doctors will use the terms small fiber polyneuropathy (SFPN) and SFN interchangeably.

At the time, I didn't understand that because small nerve fibers are found throughout the body, nerve damage can also occur in the autonomic system. The autonomic system regulates body processes that take place without a person's conscious effort. These are the processes you don't think about, because your brain manages them, whether you are asleep or awake. Some examples are heart rate, blood pressure, and body temperature. They also help manage the function of the intestines, colon, liver, pancreas, urinary tract, and reproductive system. With autonomic SFN, any of these nerve fibers can become damaged and cause a variety of symptoms. One example of an autonomic symptom is difficulty starting a stream of urine.

The symptoms of SFN can be so diverse that it is difficult to diagnose, partly because multiple organ systems are affected, and the patient is being seen by numerous specialists. The variety of symptoms can be confusing to both the patient and the doctor.

"The next step is to have a complete small fiber neuropathy work-up," Dr. Adams explained as he handed us a lab slip during a follow up appointment.

I brought Kelsey to the lab immediately, and they took vial after vial of blood. When a person has a positive skin biopsy, the doctor will order tests that look for an underlying cause, such as diabetes, systemic lupus, Fabry disease, vitamin B12 deficiency, Celiac disease, sarcoidosis, Sjogren's syndrome—to name just a few. Boston Mass General has a worksheet titled, "Tests for treatable causes of small-fiber polyneuropathy". The worksheet has 17 different blood tests. A subset on the worksheet says, "Secondary tests to consider in specific populations". This list includes ten more.

Often when someone is waiting for results, they hope everything comes back negative. But I wanted a test to come back positive, because I thought that if an underlying cause for her neuropathy was identified and treatable, then maybe we could treat the cause—and then her neuropathy symptoms could improve, and the damaged small nerve fibers could regrow.

All of Kelsey's tests came back negative, which is called idiopathic SFN. Unfortunately, this happens in 40-50% of cases. When no cause can be identified, there is no treatment. All the neurologists will do is recommend medications that might help with symptoms.

Even though her tests were negative, Dr. Adams said, "Let's try plasmapheresis. We'll put a port in her chest for regular treatments."

Plasmapheresis is basically an exchange of plasma. About 55% of a person's blood is made of plasma, which has many important roles—such as helping the body recover from injuries, distributing nutrients, removing waste, and preventing infections. During plasmapheresis, a machine is used to remove plasma containing harmful antibodies and replace it with healthy plasma.

Kelsey had just been released from the hospital. The trauma we'd experienced made us wary of medical professionals. When she was first diagnosed with vulvodynia, I got opinions from several other specialists. There was no way I was going to exchange her plasma without getting other opinions.

Next, we saw Dr. Fields, a neurologist in Boston. He said, "I wouldn't recommend plasmapheresis. She should try IVIG treatments."

IVIG stands for intravenous immunoglobulin. It is a product made up of human antibodies from the plasma of healthy donors and given intravenously in an infusion. IVIG treatments may be needed if a person isn't making enough antibodies or if their own immune system is attacking a certain type of cell or protein.

When Dr. Fields made this suggestion, Kelsey shook her head and looked scared. I explained her reaction to him. "Kelsey had one IVIG treatment in the hospital. First, she got a killer headache, and we wrapped her head in ice. Then she started hallucinating. I was sitting next to her when she asked her father to turn down the music. Her father wasn't in the room and there wasn't any music playing. I called a nurse who slowed down the rate she was receiving the IVIG."

"They probably didn't give the infusion correctly," Dr. Fields explained. "Do you know if she was premedicated? What brand of IVIG did they use?" I didn't know the answer to either of his questions and left feeling more confused.

Dr. Williams was a small fiber neuropathy expert at a different facility. I brought Kelsey there hoping he'd be the tie breaker—plasmapheresis or IVIG. He said, "I wouldn't recommend either treatment when there is no evidence that her SFN is autoimmune related."

This wasn't the answer I'd anticipated. Now I was given three different opinions. I decided to listen to Dr. Williams and do nothing, other than have Kelsey continue taking her nerve pain medications. Following Dr. Evans's advice to wear a urine bag had proven to be a terrible decision. I was afraid of making another one. In retrospect, I should have been braver and tried something. Then at least we'd have had an answer.

Despite the pain Kelsey was in, we attempted to return to our normal lives. We'd tried a vestibulectomy, pudendal nerve blocks, pelvic floor therapy, a spinal cord stimulator, and a urine bag, but nothing had changed. Her urethra still burned after she urinated. She still had difficulty starting a stream of urine and could go 24 hours being unable to get pee out. Not being able to pee normally caused sporadic UTI's.

Life would continue being interrupted without warning. I soon learned that being diagnosed with idiopathic small fiber neuropathy meant doctors would just shrug their shoulders when told her symptoms and prescribe more medications.

Before this had gotten so bad, Kelsey was a creative person. Now, without school or a job, she had nothing to occupy her time. One year for Christmas, I'd bought her everything she needed to make jewelry. There were colorful beads, wires of different sizes, strange looking tools, and books that showed various projects. We sat together at the dining room table flipping through some of the books. "Let's start with something easy," I suggested.

"What about this style?" Kelsey said as she pointed at a picture. The wire had been formed into a circle with a loop on top to string a chain through.

After we made the basic shape, Kelsey chose a pattern of colored beads to sew onto the circle with threadlike wire. For our first attempt, it looked nice, and I wore it to school on a leather chain the next day. It made Kelsey feel useful when I shared with her that I'd gotten several compliments about the necklace. We did a few other projects. But soon we found that sitting in a chair and leaning forward irritated her pelvic pain.

For months, the jewelry materials sat there unused. After walking by them countless times, I decided to give it a try myself; it would be something productive and relaxing to do on school nights instead of watching television. Soon I found I had a knack for it. My favorite project was wrapping stones with wire to create a pendant. I'd buy oval shaped stones: amethyst, tiger's eye, topaz, agate, jasper, and obsidian. Then I'd use sterling silver wire to create a bezel that held the stone in place and a bail on top to string a necklace through.

Jewelry became my escape. Wrapping a stone takes focus and concentration. When I worked on a project, I didn't think about my job or Kelsey's medical problems. Starting each day at my jewelry desk made me feel better, so it became a priority. I'd even wake up an hour earlier on a workday to make this possible. During the week, I'd look forward to working on projects over the weekends. Soon I had dozens of pendants and didn't know what to do with them all. At first, I gave them to family and friends as gifts, but then I started selling them at craft fairs. I had no intention of making a profit. I'd tally up my sales and use the money to buy more stones and wire.

At my very first craft fair, a woman walked up to my jewelry display and announced, "Today is my birthday and I'm going to buy myself a present." She took a lot of time picking up various wrapped stones, holding them up to her neck, and looking in the mirror on my table. Once a decision was made, she handed me a green colored pendant with a matching beaded necklace and a credit card.

"I'm sorry," I told her. "This is my first craft fair, and I don't have a credit card reader."

The woman was disappointed. She said, "I don't have any cash."

I hesitated for just a moment. Making the necklace had cost me over thirty dollars. Then I said, "It's your birthday. Consider this a gift."

The woman looked baffled. "Are you sure?" she asked.

I wrapped the necklace in tissue paper, placed it in a silver jewelry box, and handed it to her. "I hope you have a wonderful birthday." Making this stranger happy made me feel good. This hobby I had wanted for Kelsey had become *my* hobby—the first one I'd had time for in more than two decades.

I was due to retire from teaching in a few years. Since Brendan was in college, we no longer needed to live in the school district. Kelsey wasn't wading in the pond wearing her water shoes, and sadly, Brendan wasn't looking for frogs. I still loved our Brower Road home with its magical forest and waterfalls, but taking care of the property was monopolizing too much of our time. The plan was to move after I retired, so I wouldn't have a long commute before then.

It was the first mow of the season. Mowing the lawn could take between 7 and 8 hours. Marty was discouraged but trying to have a positive attitude. "I can do this for a few more years," he said, more to himself than to me, as he walked out the door.

Ten minutes later, he walked into the house covered with mud. The mud wasn't just on his clothes, it was in his hair and smeared on his face. "I buried the mower," he explained. "You need to drive the Ranger over so I can pull it out with a chain."

Once we got the mower free, Marty said, "I can't do this anymore. I want to move now!" In less than an hour, we'd gone from waiting three years to putting a For Sale sign in the front yard.

At first, Kelsey wasn't happy about moving from the home she grew up in. I was sad too. Change is never easy. But it was time, so we began looking for the perfect location. After months of being shown properties, we found a house we liked in a town called Broadalbin. Our new home was near shopping plazas and restaurants. It was thirty minutes from Saratoga. The Sacandaga Lake was only five minutes away.

Kelsey and I were in the car driving back from a medical appointment in Boston when Marty called and asked, "How far away are you?"

I glanced at the clock. "Still about a half hour. Why?"

"I want to show you something," Marty said, and he gave me directions.

We pulled in and found Marty in a parking lot sitting on a pontoon boat. "Come aboard," he said, as Kelsey and I climbed up the ladder.

Marty was in the driver's seat when Kelsey sat beside him. "This is great," she said. "Are you thinking about buying this boat?"

"I already did," he told her. Now we had a pontoon boat and dock space right on the Sacandaga Lake. I had loved our rowboat on the pond in Palatine Bridge, but even I had to admit this was an upgrade.

Marty and Brian both had Harley Davidson motorcycles. Occasionally Patty and I went on day trips with them. In this new location, we'd have more opportunities to go riding around the lake, and we'd be closer to the village of Lake George.

I felt bad taking Max and Marley away from the pond and woods where they'd had such fun adventures. But we fenced in the backyard at the new place, and now all we had to do was open the door and they could roam around and sit in the sun or the shade for as long as they wanted. Unlike Brower Road, our neighborhood now had sidewalks where we could take the dogs on walks around the village. Max and Marley easily adjusted to their less country-like surroundings.

Even as a young dog, Marley had sometimes yelped when he jumped from a couch or a bed to the floor. Then he'd lie there for hours without moving. X-rays showed he had degeneration in his back discs. The vet said this was abnormal for a dog his age and had to be a genetic problem. We'd always had pain meds and anti-inflammatories on hand for him. Luckily this only happened occasionally, and with a bit of rest and meds, he was fine.

But one evening, when Marley was about 10, we came home and found him lying on the floor with his back legs spread out behind him. He was in a state of panic because he couldn't stand up or move. Kelsey and I lay on the floor next to him all night doing our best to keep him calm and as comfortable as possible.

In the morning, Marty lifted him into the car. I said a tearful goodbye to Marley, feeling quite certain that he wouldn't be coming home. Kelsey and Marty took him to the vet, where he was diagnosed with a pinched nerve that paralyzed him. There was no recovery.

Marley was put to sleep that day. When they got home, Kelsey went to her room and cried for days. She could barely look at anyone without bursting into tears.

About a week later, I went to the vet's office and retrieved the ceramic container holding Marley's ashes. There was also a plaster circle with his paw print and name on it. None of us was ready to decide what to do with the ashes, so I put them in a cabinet.

This was a great loss for all of us, but especially for Kelsey. We had always told her that she'd saved Marley, and how lucky we were that she brought him into our lives. For the first time in eighteen years, we had only one dog, Max, who I would forever see as a puppy in the mall being held in Kelsey's arms.

Chapter Twelve

Kelsey started having symptoms unrelated to her urinary tract. Being nauseated became commonplace, and sometimes she vomited even though she wasn't truly sick. A motility test showed that over a four-day period, the food she ate barely moved through her digestive tract. Doctors called this colonic inertia, and it caused severe constipation. During a colonoscopy, a gastroenterologist found abnormal dilation throughout her colon, which made bowel movements painful. Kelsey was always too hot or too cold, never comfortable. When small fiber neuropathy affects the nerves in the autonomic system, it can cause all these problems.

Now, during a 24-hour period, Kelsey slept more than she was awake. She could have a drink in her hand and fall asleep before it reached her mouth. Then the liquid would spill in her lap. One day I handed Kelsey a plate of scrambled eggs, which tended to be soothing to her stomach. While she tried to eat this single meal, I had to wake her up four different times. If we left the house for a medical appointment, it would take her days to recover from overwhelming fatigue.

In a lecture given by a Mass General neurologist, the doctor explained why people with small fiber neuropathy can find fatigue to be a crippling symptom. Muscles have blood vessels inside them that are lined with small nerve fibers. These blood vessels open and close to provide the muscles with oxygen and nutrients. When a person lacks these fibers, the blood vessels can't open and close properly, so the muscles don't get what they need to function. This causes exercise intolerance, muscle weakness, chronic fatigue, and shortness of breath.

Sometimes, in those days, I thought back to when Kelsey had run, played softball, been athletic. She'd especially loved to swim, spending hours in the ocean on vacations, excited to be anywhere that had a pool. Being in saltwater or chlorinated water now, if she could even get to it, made her typical burning pain much worse. Our trip to Arizona in 2015 was the last time I saw her swim without issue. After a few bad encounters, Kelsey had decided it wasn't worth the risk and had given up swimming entirely.

We went to see Dr. Larson, a neurologist in Manhattan, and went over this huge list of symptoms with her. She said, "I really don't think Kelsey has small fiber neuropathy."

I replied, "That would be great. Why don't you repeat the biopsy?"

She agreed and did another skin punch test. I received a call from her a couple of weeks later. "I was wrong," she said. "I'm sorry to tell you that Kelsey definitely has small fiber neuropathy." The second biopsy showed a nerve fiber density of 0.4 in Kelsey's thigh; an abnormal result is less than 8.3. The nerve fiber density in her calf was 1.3; an abnormal result there is less than 6.4. This was significantly worse than the first biopsy, showing progression with even more nerve fibers being damaged.

The neurologist had questioned this diagnosis because Kelsey wasn't the typical SFN patient. An article published in 2019 in *NIH Pub Med National Library of Medicine* titled "Complex Chronic Pelvic Pain Linked to Small Fiber Polyneuropathy" best describes why patients like Kelsey shouldn't be overlooked. In the Mass General study, sixty-four percent of patients with chronic pelvic pain were found to have SFPN. These patients described having pain with a full bladder, urethral pain during and after urination, pain on the vulvar surface and vaginal pain during sexual activity. The study also linked SFPN to reflux disease, fibromyalgia, migraine, irritable bowel syndrome, lower back pain, interstitial cystitis, endometriosis, and even vulvodynia. These patients had abnormal voiding studies, and some had difficulty starting a stream of urine.

Kelsey saw doctors from gynecology, urology, genetics, pulmonology, rheumatology, pain management, and gastroenterology. Within the gastro field, there was a doctor to monitor her pancreas, and another called a motility expert. These specialists didn't communicate with each other, so none of her care was ever coordinated. They didn't treat Kelsey like a human being who had systems that were all connected and not working.

I always believed that if I found the right doctor, the right facility, or the right treatment, eventually I would "fix" Kelsey. While she was growing up, I never doubted this for a second. In my mind it was a simple fact that required patience and perseverance. It was my job as her mother to never give up. The answer was out there somewhere, and it was my responsibility to find it.

I'm not sure when I started to have doubts, but I no longer believed this to be true. Kelsey kept getting worse, not better. Every medical treatment had failed. Each path I'd gone down was the wrong path. Maybe this situation was out of my control, and she'd be in pain for the rest of her life. Coming to this realization was devastating. Even after the small fiber neuropathy diagnosis, I still thought Kelsey had a chance of her symptoms improving, of her finding a part-time job and someday getting married.

People at work used to ask me how Kelsey was doing. I'd share our plans for an upcoming appointment and what I hoped the doctor would do for her. We got to a point where I ran out of ideas. There was no plan. Now when colleagues asked how she was doing, I'd get teary and tell them how bad the situation had become. They stopped asking. If I couldn't make Kelsey better, I worried, how could she survive in this world without us? I was used to sleepless nights, but now I started to worry—what will happen to Kelsey when we're gone?

"Maybe I should ask a doctor about going on disability," Kelsey suggested. Without any income, she had to ask us for everything she wanted or needed. Instead of relying on her parents, she hoped this financial assistance would give her some independence.

I wasn't ready to consider this option. Once Kelsey was viewed as a disabled person, I thought there'd be no turning back. I resisted this idea for quite some time, but eventually gave in and made an appointment with yet another doctor. He interviewed Kelsey and read her medical history.

"The case has to go through a review board," the doctor explained. "But I'm recommending your disability gets approved." He considered this to be good news and gave Kelsey a fatherly smile. I left feeling like a failure.

Receiving these payments wasn't the solution any of us thought it would be. It amounted to a little over $500 dollars a month–enough for her car payment and insurance, plus a little bit left over for spending money. It was nice, but it didn't make me sleep better or worry less about her future.

There was a house twenty minutes from us that belonged to Marty's side of the family. His aunt and uncle who'd once lived there had both passed away many years ago. Now, we thought maybe we could renovate it for Kelsey. It had ancient plumbing, unsafe electrical work, and windows that needed replacing. We had no idea how much such a project would cost.

On the plus side, Marty's brother and his family lived on the same road, so she wouldn't be alone. Also, the house was close enough that we could continue providing Kelsey with the care and assistance she needed. She was 26 now, and I wanted her to learn some life skills and become more independent. Just thinking she'd have a place to live when we were gone gave me some peace of mind. This could be her forever home.

Marty said, "Let's start with the septic tank. If that goes well, we'll consider renovating the rest of the house."

A septic company met Marty at the property while I was at work. I called to see how things went. "Once we got the lid open," Marty explained, "the entire tank collapsed."

For the next week, we weighed the pros and cons of renovating. One day we'd feel positive and think it was a good idea. The next day we'd think we were crazy because there was an enormous amount of work to be done. And knowing Marty and me, we wouldn't just make the house acceptable, we'd make it the best it could be. Even though the house failed our initial test, we decided to proceed. The first thing we did was replace the septic tank.

Kelsey had never been inside the house on Knowlton Road. Before starting this huge project, we took her there for a walk-through. Marty opened the door into the mudroom, which had no Sheetrock, only framing with exposed electrical wires. "After replacing all the electrical work," he explained, "we'll close up these walls."

Next, we walked into an empty kitchen. Marty said, "We'll install cabinets, get new appliances, and replace the flooring."

We continued going from room to room sharing our vision with Kelsey, but now, electrical wires came through drilled holes in the floor. Filthy blue carpeting covered the downstairs. Upstairs was linoleum flooring from the 1960's. The cast iron sink and tub were permanently stained a nasty brown color. At the top of the stairs was a railing that shook if you were foolish enough to put your hand on it. The house looked scary, like a possible location for a horror movie. I expected Kelsey to be frightened that we thought someday she would live here. In its current state, the house was unlivable.

Instead, Kelsey was thrilled. She said, "I can't believe you guys are giving me a house!"

At the end of the tour, I told her, "You aren't allowed back inside until the renovations are finished. Then we'll have a reveal party like they have on TV."

The first step was to demo much of the existing house. One day, at work, I opened my phone to a photo of Marty with a severely swollen cheek and abrasions all over his face. "I'm okay," said his accompanying message. He had crawled underneath thc 100-pound cast iron sink while attempting to remove it, and, once the heavy structure shifted, it became unstable and fell on his head, a pipe just missing his eye. A week later, trying to remove the stained tub, he hit his thumb with a sledgehammer. For weeks his thumb was bandaged, bruised, and swollen.

I thought maybe we'd gotten ourselves into a situation we weren't qualified for.

We persevered. Getting the water tested was a priority. On my way home from work, I stopped at the house to wait for the water guy. When I opened the door to the basement and hit the light switch at the top of the stairs, nothing happened. I called Marty. He said, "That switch doesn't work. You need to go in the basement, reach up, and twist the lightbulb."

It was pouring outside, with no sunlight. The stairway was dark, so I used the flashlight on my phone to guide the way. The basement walls were made from actual stone placed more than one-hundred years ago; the floor was mostly dirt. We had left the basement off Kelsey's tour list, and I had never found it necessary to venture down here before.

At the bottom of the stairs, I stood in a huge puddle, reached up, and put my hand on a lightbulb dangling from the ceiling. For just a moment, I hesitated—water, electricity, not a great combination. Call it faith or stupidity: I twisted the bulb, the light came on, and I ran up the stairs.

We hired professionals to replace the electrical work, plumbing, and windows. Marty was an experienced painter. He painted all the rooms, many with the same colors as our house so it would feel familiar to Kelsey. I wasn't a great painter, but I painted the mudroom, sunporch, doors, and the elaborate molding found in older homes. All ten rooms got new vinyl flooring.

Now we had a beautiful house, but it was empty. We searched for used furniture that was in great shape. I hung family photos on the walls and framed Kelsey's favorite pictures to display on shelves. Curtains and throw rugs added color and made the house feel cozy. My favorite room was the sunporch, where two of the exterior walls were all windows. I spray painted an old wicker furniture set to look like new. The couch, table, and rocking chair made the sunporch look inviting. On Kelsey's birthday, she opened boxes filled with dishes, silverware, bedsheets, and bathroom towels. Renovating the house from top to bottom took over a year.

In November of 2020, it was time for the big reveal. Family and friends gathered at the house about thirty minutes before Kelsey and Marty were due to arrive. When Kelsey walked into her new home for the first time, she was overwhelmed and could barely speak. Just as we had initially done, we took her from room to room. "I love it! Oh wow, I love it!" she kept repeating. "The house doesn't look anything like it did before." And she was right. As a housewarming gift, I'd made her a photo album filled with before and after pictures.

At the end of the party, Kelsey walked her guests to the door. "Goodbye, thank you for coming," she said proudly. It was the first time she was the hostess in a place of her own. That night, she slept in her new bedroom. I stayed there too, thinking she'd be afraid. I planned to stay longer, but the next day, she said, "Mom, I love it here and I'm not scared. You can go home. I'll be fine." Leaving her there alone, without me to take care of her, was harder than I anticipated. Now our two extra bedrooms were empty and available for guests, although we still referred to them as Brendan's room and Kelsey's room. I also had a little more space and quiet around me, which meant I could read even more than usual.

For as long as I could remember, reading had been a source of comfort. I'd pick up a fictional story that might be suspenseful, dramatic, or show how two people fell in love, and I'd escape into it. When Kelsey was about 16 and her illness started taking over our lives, I stopped reading fiction–in part because these stories weren't about real people with real problems. Instead, I started reading nonfiction books and soon discovered memoirs. In the ones I found most memorable, something awful happened to the author, but then their struggle led them in a new and positive direction. These books were my favorites because they taught lessons about life.

To some people this might sound strange. Why would anyone enjoy reading about awful things happening to people? To me, while a part of their story was sad, I found the author's journey after the tragedy to be inspiring. Their experience showed their resilience; it made them admirably stronger. This type of memoir gave me what I was searching for—proof that something good could come from something bad.

Whether we were in a doctor's waiting room or the hospital, or when Kelsey was having a procedure or getting a pudendal nerve block, I always had whatever book I was reading at the time stashed in my purse. I'd tell her about the book in as much detail as she wanted. I hoped these inspirational stories would encourage her not to give up. I was always trying to convince her that someday she'd find her own something good.

Just a couple of months after she moved in, Kelsey and I were sitting on the couch in her living room. "I read a book a few years ago and told you all about it," I reminded her. "This young man barely left his apartment because he had so many medical problems. Then he got a dog from an animal shelter, and the dog changed his life. Dad and I want to get you a puppy, if you want one."

Kelsey couldn't believe it. "Yes! My own puppy!" she exclaimed. "I wanted a dog, but I never thought I'd get one this soon."

I had done some research ahead of time. I said, "A basset hound would be a good choice. They barely need any exercise."

Kelsey was disappointed. "I really want a lab or a golden retriever." This didn't surprise me, because these were the breeds she'd grown up with.

"They're not low-energy dogs," I said, knowing that she wouldn't be able to give a dog like this enough exercise. But I wanted her to be happy, and I knew that taking care of a dog would give her a purpose— and a companion. When I left work, I drove by her house on my way home, so I stopped there all the time. It would be easy for me to help walk the dog. And a golden retriever would be an excellent roommate.

I soon found a woman who had been breeding these dogs for more than twenty years. When I told her about Kelsey's health problems, she said, "I have a litter available in March with huge parents and another litter available in April with much smaller parents." I put a deposit down on a male puppy available in April. We certainly didn't need a huge golden retriever.

In the memoir I'd read, the man could walk the dog for only a block or two in the beginning. Over time, he got stronger, and soon he could walk the dog for miles. As he walked, people asked him questions about his beautiful, friendly dog. These people became his friends, and soon he had a social life. I hoped this puppy would help Kelsey become more active and improve her quality of life, just like the man in the book.

Kelsey was trying to decide on a name for the puppy and had narrowed the choices down to fifteen, which were all written on a sheet of paper. She was saying them aloud as if she were calling an imaginary dog, "Teddy, Jackson, Brody, Jake!" Then she said, "I think I should meet the puppy before giving him a name."

I reminded her that when she was in the New Visions Health program in high school, her favorite placement was the nursing home. "You'd come home and tell me about the people you met, how lonely they were, and how much you enjoyed spending time with them," I told her. "When the puppy gets older, you could train him to become a therapy dog."

"That would be the perfect job for me," Kelsey said. She was thrilled about this idea. "Then we could visit people who are in pain like me and make them feel better."

By Easter time, we had to wait just two more weeks before we could bring the puppy home. I still enjoyed making Kelsey and Brendan Easter baskets, especially when, this year, I could make her basket dog-themed. Inside I put a blue leash, a matching collar, two bags of dog treats, a stuffed animal, and a package of small chewing bones. We eagerly counted down the days until April 18th.

When the day finally arrived, Kelsey and I drove to the breeder's house. We knocked on the door and could barely contain our excitement when we heard dogs barking. The breeder showed us a doggy playpen with two male golden retriever puppies.

"They're so tiny and adorable," Kelsey said as she reached down and held a puppy in her arms.

I picked up the other puppy and said, "I can't believe how much bigger Max was at this age."

Kelsey and I kept trading the puppies back and forth. Then we set them on the floor and watched them play. They both had dark soulful eyes, big floppy ears, and soft golden puppy fur.

"How am I ever going to choose?" Kelsey said. I knew which one I would choose, but I stayed quiet, of course. Kelsey held each puppy a few more times and stared into their eyes. Finally, she said, "I want this one."

Once in the car, I told Kelsey she had chosen the puppy I was secretly rooting for. He was born on February 22, 2021, and weighed only 7 pounds. Kelsey named him Brody. As I drove, she had him snuggled in a blanket asleep on her chest.

When we got back to the house, Brody peed in the grass before Kelsey carried him inside. She took off the leash so he could explore his new home. He first discovered his water dish and eagerly drank after the long car ride. Kelsey got biscuits from the treat jar and tossed them into the dog crate to show him it was a safe place. Brody didn't hesitate to run inside and eat them. Next, we scattered an assortment of toys we'd already bought for him on the floor. Brody chose a stuffed lamb and plopped down on his new dog bed. We laughed at how he immediately looked at home, comfortable and content. It was impossible to look at him and not smile. Kelsey looked the happiest I'd seen her in years.

Chapter Thirteen

Over the next six weeks, Kelsey and I took Brody to puppy classes. He excelled at his homework and easily learned to sit, stay, lie down, and shake paws when asked. Kelsey could put a treat on the floor and say, "Leave it." Then she'd leave the room, and Brody wouldn't eat the treat until she returned and said, "Okay." You only needed to practice a new command two or three times for him to learn it.

We fenced in the backyard, so all Kelsey had to do was open the sun porch door to let Brody out. This helped a great deal with his endless puppy energy. We could throw him a frisbee, a ball, and he could spend time outdoors getting fresh air.

When it got warmer, Kelsey and I took Brody to a beach on the lake with me in my swimsuit. I carried him out until the water was up to my waist, then set him down.

Kelsey stayed on the shore and shouted, "Come Brody, come!"

Brody's little legs started paddling towards Kelsey as fast as they could. Once he reached the shore, Kelsey lifted him up, gave him a hug, and said, "Good boy." We did this a few more times until Brody swam to her with more confidence.

On a gorgeous summer day, Marty called Kelsey. "Let's take Brody out on the boat and have dinner," he said. "What kind of sandwich would you like?"

Brody was excited and curious as he approached the dock, but he wasn't happy about those mysterious gaps between the boards, which he'd never seen before. Instead of looking ahead, he stared down at his feet, walking cautiously, as if he thought he might slip between the cracks. A foot of water stood between him and the boat. He refused to take that leap, so Kelsey picked him up and placed him on the floor.

When Marty started the motor, Brody heard this loud noise and froze. He didn't seem to be enjoying himself, but I'd seen Max have these same reactions and knew it was only a matter of time before he relaxed. Once the boat started moving, Brody's curiosity overcame his fear. He started wandering around, looking over the side of the boat at the water, and raising his head to feel the cool breeze on his face.

"I think he likes it," Kelsey said. She picked Brody up, held him against her cheek, and said, "Mom, take our picture."

Marty turned the motor off so we could float around while eating our sandwiches. Brody had been drinking a lot of water from all the excitement. "I think we should head back before he pees," I suggested.

While Marty was putting the cover on the boat, Kelsey and I took Brody over to the shoreline and threw a stick in the water. He eagerly walked in, but as soon as the ground disappeared beneath his feet, he ran back without the stick.

Kelsey laughed. "It's okay, Brody, you can do it!" She found another stick and threw it closer, trying to entice him.

Brody couldn't resist the temptation. He swam through the water and brought the stick back, just as you would expect a retriever to do. Kelsey threw the stick a few more times, each time a little farther out. Brody became braver, swam in the deeper water, and retrieved the stick.

Whenever possible, Kelsey and I included Brody rather than leaving him at home in his crate. This meant he came with us for certain appointments such as the dentist, who Kelsey saw frequently. Her teeth were rapidly decaying, another symptom no one could explain. The enamel that was supposed to be protecting her teeth had just suddenly disappeared. While Kelsey was with the dentist, Brody and I walked around the village of Schoharie. This was great multitasking. When Kelsey was finished, she'd give me a call, and then Brody and I would meet her back at the car.

One day in early October, when it was still warm enough to wear a T-shirt and shorts, Kelsey and I took Brody to Wintergreen Park in Canajoharie. He was eight months old, and this was his first time going for a walk in the woods. There are steep cliffs along the gorge, so we were careful to keep him close on a leash. We walked to the end of the trail to see the forty-foot waterfall from the wooden observation deck. Kelsey kept posing with Brody and having me take their picture.

"He's loving this!" Kelsey exclaimed. Seeing him happy made her happy.

Just as I'd hoped, Brody was giving Kelsey a purpose. She was still having terrible nights, burning urination, painful bowel movements, and chronic fatigue. It had taken three tries before we'd made it to Wintergreen Park. We would plan on going, then she'd have a sleepless night or didn't feel well, and we'd reschedule. But having Brody inspired her to participate in life when she was having a better day. I felt relieved. My plan was working.

But the change of seasons brought colder weather. During the summer months, Kelsey had put Brody in her car and walked him on a nearby bike path. Now this path was bitter cold, windy, or covered with ice and snow. There was no easy way to walk Brody from Kelsey's house; on one side was a heavily trafficked road with no sidewalk, and in the other direction was a long, steep hill. I was concerned that Kelsey might fall if she tried to walk Brody up or down this slope when it, too, was often covered with ice and snow. That winter, Brody and I carefully navigated the slippery hill while Kelsey barely left the house.

I had retired from teaching, which should have made it easier to take care of Kelsey and Brody. But it didn't feel that way, because I started feeling sorry for myself. Now, I wasn't naturally going by Kelsey's house after work anymore on my way home; I had to make a point to go. I still went all the time, because she needed me—and now Brody needed me, too. While driving there, I'd try to have a positive attitude, but I was really thinking, *I don't want to do this for the rest of my life.* After teaching for 33 years, I was excited to be retired and have all the freedom that comes with the title. My daughter was now 28, my son 25. I felt like I was in a place where I should finally have some time for myself—to make more jewelry, have lunch with friends on a weekday, or stay in my pajamas and read a book.

It seems foolish now when I reflect on my thinking process. When I was renovating the house for Kelsey, I kept imagining what her life would be like. I pictured her standing at the stove making dinner, having friends over to visit, sleeping in her bedroom at night, and waking up in the morning, as healthy people do. But this is not what Kelsey's life had been like before. Why did I think the house was going to magically make everything better?

The doctors couldn't fix Kelsey; her having a home didn't help the way I had imagined. Now, Brody wasn't making at least some of the changes in her life that I'd hoped for. Now, when I looked at Kelsey, I felt so much emotional pain that sometimes it caused physical symptoms. My heart would pound, and I might get short of breath or start shaking. I'd feel the need to get away, like a panic attack.

My solution was to put up a protective wall that felt like a forcefield. I thought this would make things easier; then, when I looked at Kelsey, it wouldn't hurt as much. But instead, it made things worse, because a part of me had shut down. My strength, resilience, and compassion disappeared. I had done everything I could possibly think of to save my daughter, and it—I—had had failed. Walking into Kelsey's house now triggered an overwhelming sense of anger, and I became a person neither of us recognized.

At Kelsey's, I'd usually find her asleep on the living room couch. She'd stir a bit, sensing my presence, but her eyes would stay shut. This is when my attempt to have a positive attitude would fail. It made me angry that she most likely would spend the rest of her life asleep on the couch. I missed looking into her brilliant blue eyes, which were now dull and gray. As a young girl, she was vibrant and always ready to have fun. What had happened to my daughter? How did we get here?

While she slept, I'd start stomping around like a petulant child, letting Brody out, picking up clothes that were lying around, washing dishes she'd left in the sink. The noise I was making usually got her attention.

"Mom is that you?" she'd ask from a foggy, mindless state.

I'd return to the living room with my head down, shoulders raised with tension, and mouth closed, firm and straight.

Kelsey would look at me confused and say, "I see you hunching up your shoulders. Why are you mad? You just got here."

I'd take a deep breath, trying to calm myself.

She'd say, "I was up all night trying to go to the bathroom. I'm exhausted." Then she'd close her eyes and fall back to sleep.

If she managed to stay awake while I was there, I would criticize her about everything, rather than asking her how she felt or taking a stab at a normal conversation. "You didn't fill your pill tray," I'd admonish. "Now you're going to run out of two medications before I can fill them." This tirade would continue, and I'd go on and on telling her all the things she wasn't doing. When I left, I'm sure she was glad to see me go.

I was mad because I wanted to walk in my daughter's house to find her showered, dressed, and ready to start the day. I wanted to say things like, "Let's go have lunch," or "Let's go shopping!" I selfishly wondered what I had done to deserve this. I knew, of course, that Kelsey would never choose to live like this, but my anger made me impatient and short-tempered. I started treating Kelsey like a patient instead of my daughter. The mom she once knew, had known all her life, was gone, and in her place was an irritable caretaker.

Kelsey always said, "I love you," as I left the house, even if she was half asleep.

I said, "I love you too," which of course I did. But I said it in more of an exasperated way.

On the drive home, I'd be disappointed in myself. I'd call Kelsey from the car and tell her I was sorry. I didn't have to say what for, it was obvious.

Kelsey could tell I was struggling. She'd say, "It's okay Mom, I understand."

This scene kept repeating itself. When I was short-tempered and impatient, Kelsey was kind and forgiving. I was aware of this cycle and kept trying to break it, but I couldn't find a way. It felt like we had switched places. I was angry at the world Kelsey lived in because I didn't have control and couldn't fix it. Meanwhile, she was the one showing me unconditional love.

I explained to Marty what was happening. I told him, "I feel perfectly fine, but then the moment I walk into her house, this anger takes over me. Even though I know it's about to happen, I can't stop it."

He said, "Maybe you should talk to a counselor and ask for help." I thought this was great advice, but the last thing I needed was another appointment.

Winter was finally coming to an end. With nice weather, I thought, *I'll get Kelsey outside, we'll do things with Brody, and I'll get better.* After being indoors for months, Kelsey was also looking forward to warmer days and outdoor activities.

But then a new symptom started. Kelsey said, "I'm having trouble swallowing. It feels like my pills are getting stuck in my throat."

We went to an ear, nose, and throat (ENT) doctor who did a laryngeal flexible endoscopic examination. Basically, this is a thin flexible tube with a camera at the end that allows the doctor to view the pharynx and larynx. The first time she did the scope, Dr. Torres found swelling, which she called edema, in a few locations. When Kelsey's symptoms persisted, we returned to the ENT doctor just two weeks later. Dr. Torres repeated the scope and found inflammation and significant changes with edema in multiple locations, including the vocal cords.

She sent Kelsey for a barium swallow test. During this test, X-ray images were taken as Kelsey swallowed. The results showed several esophageal tertiary contractions—somewhat unusual for her age.

Dr. Torres tried to explain. She said, "The muscles in your esophagus aren't squeezing in a sequential manner, as they should. Instead, your muscles are squeezing randomly." She demonstrated this using a closed fist. In the first example, she overlapped her fists in a straight line. Then she squeezed her fists sporadically to show what Kelsey's esophagus was doing. Dr. Torres attributed this problem to her small fiber neuropathy. Kelsey was terribly uncomfortable, but the doctor seemed unconcerned.

About a year before, Marty and I had planned a motorcycle trip with Brian and Patty. Going away was never easy, but this new symptom made me more worried than usual. Before we left, I made sure Kelsey had everything she needed. I counted out her meds, got her groceries, cleaned her house, and made sure Brody had enough dog food. My mom made Kelsey promise to check in with her everyday while I was gone.

Marty and Brian loaded two Harley Davidson motorcycles onto a trailer. Then the four of us got in a truck that pulled the trailer to South Dakota—two 12-hour days of driving each way—where we'd rented a house for a week. Each morning, we headed out for a ride to see the Midwest—the men driving, Patty and me passengers. We drove the motorcycles through Spearfish Canyon, Needles Highway, and Badlands National Park.

One day we rode to Wyoming and hiked around Devils Tower, a rock that's over 800 feet tall. While walking, my phone rang. The moment I saw Kelsey's name, I panicked and answered, without saying hello, "Is something wrong?"

"Everything is fine," Kelsey said. "I just wanted to give you a call."

I felt instant relief. "How are you feeling?"

"I'm doing okay," she told me.

It was a short conversation, probably because we were both pretending. Whenever I went away, Kelsey wanted me to relax and not worry about her, so she'd tell me she was okay even when she wasn't. In turn, I pretended to believe her because I knew she didn't want me to ask her questions. This was a silly game we had perfected over the years; once I got home, she'd tell me how awful she'd really felt in my absence.

Along the trail, we noticed pieces of cloth tied to tree branches. Then we read about this tradition on a plaque. Native Americans tied these cloths to represent a person making an offering or a request, or in remembrance of a person. They are referred to as prayer cloths. I didn't know this at the time, but hikers aren't supposed to participate in this activity meant only for those with Native American heritage.

Marty asked, "Do you want to say a prayer for Kelsey?"

"I had the same thought," I said, and I gave him my headband to use as a prayer cloth.

It felt fitting to use something personal. We chose a tree, and Marty climbed on a rock. He tied my headband to a branch. Then we stood quietly and said a prayer for Kelsey. I prayed for her to have less pain and a better future.

When we got back from our trip, Kelsey said, "It feels like a metal chain is being dragged through my throat. My mouth is so dry that my teeth feel like plastic. There's a strange pressure coming from the top of my head but it's nothing like a headache." I found this onslaught of new symptoms baffling.

Brody and I returned from a walk one day to find Kelsey on the couch looking pale and nauseated. I said, "Maybe it isn't safe for you to live alone right now. Why don't you come home and stay with us for a few weeks?"

Kelsey looked mortified. She said, "No way. I'm staying in my own house with Brody."

Of course, Brody would have come too. I thought maybe I should ask Marty to talk to her, but I let it go. She was adamant about staying.

Every couple of years, I asked Dr. Williams to repeat the lab testing for causes of small fiber neuropathy. Idiopathic—which means the cause is unknown—was unacceptable to me. I always believed that with time, the cause would reveal itself.

Marty and I were on the boat when the results came through on the patient portal. I said, "Kelsey just tested positive on an Early Sjogren's Panel." I felt such relief that I started to cry. Maybe we finally knew the cause of her SFN. Even though there's no cure for Sjogren's, I thought that maybe now Kelsey could get the help she needed to better manage her symptoms.

Sjogren's syndrome is a chronic autoimmune disorder that happens when the immune system attacks the glands that make moisture in the eyes, mouth, and other parts of the body. Because Sjogren's attacks the salivary glands, people with this disease often experience severe tooth decay. Other symptoms include difficulty swallowing, slow motility (constipation), fatigue, and even vulvodynia.

Kelsey had previously tested negative for the typical Sjogren's antibodies. While waiting for these antibodies to appear, Sjogren patients can have on average a three-year delay in being properly diagnosed. This is a recent improvement, as it used to take six years. Now, researchers have identified biomarkers found in early Sjogren's and developed a test for them. The John Hopkins Center directed me to a Sjogren's specialist in Rochester, NY. I took the next available appointment, at the end of October.

We'd been discouraged from trying intravenous immunoglobulin (IVIG) infusions because Kelsey had never showed an autoimmune problem on her lab tests. Sjogren's was the evidence we needed, so I called the neurologist. His next available appointment was nine months away. I asked if we could get IVIG approval before the appointment, since Kelsey was already diagnosed with SFN. No, I was told. I took the appointment, thinking we've waited this long to try IVIG, we'll just have to wait the nine months to discuss this with the neurologist. And in the meantime, we'd ask the Sjogren's specialist for his opinion.

During a lecture, I'd written down the name of a doctor in Boston who specialized in treating the chronic fatigue associated with SFN. Now, I called his office as well. The next available appointment for him was in April, and it got added to the calendar. When all this happened, we were already waiting to see a new gastroenterologist in September. Seeing these four doctors gave me a sense of hope that I hadn't felt in a long time.

*   *   *

By the end of summer, Kelsey was extremely frustrated. Brody and I were going on walks to the marsh trail without her. She didn't get to go on the boat with Brody, as she had last year. We never made a return trip to Wintergreen Park, as planned. Soon it would be cold again. Once more, she'd missed out on everything.

I was frustrated too, which perpetuated the cycle of anger I was experiencing. The nice weather was supposed to make everything better, but it didn't. I was annoyed that Kelsey wouldn't get off the couch, even though I knew that she virtually couldn't. Instead of encouraging her in a positive way, I was criticizing her efforts, which only made things worse.

Along with the ENT doctor, Kelsey had gone to the Emergency Room three times in the past five months complaining of severe abdominal and rectal pain. We were once again in the car when Kelsey said, "Something is seriously wrong with me. People are going to be sorry. There will be a reckoning."

I was startled by this grave declaration. She didn't say this in an angry or mean-spirited way, but rather calmly, as a matter of fact. I said, "Kelsey, you're going to be fine. You've seen a lot of doctors lately and everyone says you're okay."

I caught myself, took a breath, and tried to be encouraging. "You're seeing a new gastro doctor. You have appointments with a Sjogren's and a chronic fatigue specialist. The neurologist will prescribe IVIG treatments." I was thinking, *Just hold on, we finally have a plan I think is promising.* Of course, I'd thought this many times before and had always been wrong.

Reckoning was such an unusual word for Kelsey to use. Even though I knew the meaning of this word, that night I looked up the definition. It means a time when someone's actions will be judged to be right or wrong so they may be punished accordingly. What Kelsey said in the car really bothered me.

If I didn't go to Kelsey's house on a particular day, I always checked on her. We'd been together for most of that Monday. On Tuesday, I was working at a store in Albany where my jewelry was for sale. I texted Kelsey in the afternoon to remind her that she had an online appointment. When she didn't respond, I called, but she didn't answer. I started calling every ten minutes for an hour, but still no answer.

At 3:00, I called Marty. "Kelsey missed her on-line appointment and isn't answering her phone," I explained. "Can you go check on her?"

Marty said, "Sure, I'm still at the college." Kelsey's house was only ten minutes from there. Around 4:00, he called me back. "Kelsey is in the bathroom having a lot of pain. I asked if she wanted me to stay, but she said no."

This wasn't unusual. When Kelsey was in pain, she preferred to be alone. After work, I considered canceling my dinner plans and going to Kelsey's house, but I decided to just call her when we were done. As I drove home, she wasn't answering her phone again. I was relieved when she finally answered, just as I was getting into bed.

"I'm in a lot of pain," she said. "I love you." She hung up before I could say anything.

I thought, *If I drive over there, what can I do?* She'd probably be up all night trying to go to the bathroom. Knowing I'd see her in the morning, I decided to go to sleep.

Chapter Fourteen

The next morning was sunny and surprisingly warm for late September. I took Max for a walk around the village before heading over to Kelsey's house. On the backseat of my car was a laundry basket filled with her recently washed clothes; we hadn't yet installed a washer or dryer at her place, so I took her laundry to my home and did it for her.

With the laundry basket balanced on my hip, I unlocked the door into the mudroom. Next came the kitchen door, but when I turned the knob, it was locked. I stood there for a moment, confused; Kelsey and I never locked this door. Then I remembered Marty was here yesterday. He must have locked it when he left. I set the laundry basket down to get the keys back out of my purse.

I set one foot into the kitchen, then froze, immediately noticing something was out of place. To my right, there'd normally be a clear view through the dining room into the living room, but something was on the floor. At first, I wasn't sure what it was. It looked…well, it looked like Kelsey. But it couldn't be, because the skin on this person was dark gray. Not a normal skin color. Not a color I'd ever seen on a person. She was lying on the floor with her head bent against the wall at a strange angle.

I dropped the laundry basket and ran in—because of course it was Kelsey. It was my daughter, lying there on the floor. *Maybe she's just hurt*, I thought. *She probably just fell!* But as I ran, I knew better. A merely hurt person wouldn't look like that. Something was horribly wrong.

The moment I was facing Kelsey from the front, not the side, I could see her eyes. They were open: looking at me, but not seeing.

And then I knew. I knew instantly from that vacant stare—my daughter was gone. Yet even as I knew this, my mind resisted. I grabbed her bent arm that stood unnaturally on its own in the air and shook her hard. "Kelsey!" I shouted. "Kelsey!" The arm I held was stiff and cold, yet a part of me wanted to believe she was just sleeping.

I was focused on Kelsey, but then I saw something move. It was Brody. He jumped off the couch and came over, as if he now realized something was wrong. Then he lay down across her lap and waited for her to notice him, but of course she didn't. "Kelsey!" I yelled once more. Neither one of us could wake her.

What I was seeing was too much to bear, something no parent should ever have to witness. I wanted the image to go away, so I turned and ran from the living room, outside, and onto the lawn. My mind told my body not to stop. I needed to keep moving, to keep running forever, but I didn't know where to go. So I ran in circles, looking up at the sky and screaming, "She's dead. She's dead. She's dead."

I'm not sure how long I did this. I couldn't think. I almost couldn't breathe. All I could do was yell and keep moving, around and around.

Eventually, somehow, I remembered my brother-in-law's house up the hill. Still yelling, I ran in that direction. When I got there, I banged on the door. No one answered. I banged again, and again. It had taken me so long to get here, to make this single decision, and now I was still alone, no idea what to do.

I ran back down the hill. Only then did it occur to me to call 911. With shaking hands, I pressed the buttons on my phone. A woman answered. I gasped for air as I tried to speak. I said, "I walked into my daughter's house and she's dead."

The woman said, "Do you need an ambulance?"

"No!" I shouted into the phone. "She's dead."

"Okay Ma'am," said the woman. "I'll send someone there right away, but I need you to tell me the address. Can you give that to me?"

Something this simple wasn't easy for me to answer. I had to glance at the mailbox before giving her the house number.

A neighbor who lived a few houses down the road was walking toward me now, as I approached Kelsey's driveway again. "I heard someone screaming," she said, as she got a little closer. "Is everything okay?"

My body shook violently. I shouted, "I went into my daughter's house and she's dead."

The neighbor turned pale. "Oh my god," she said. "Are you—do you need me to call 911?"

"I called," I told her. "They're coming."

"I'm so sorry," she said. "Let me help."

My legs gave out then as she reached for me. I sat down in Kelsey's driveway, leaning against my car. The neighbor sat beside me. We stayed there until the police car pulled in. Then I got up and ran to the officer. I told him, "I went into my daughter's house and she's dead."

He nodded, then walked toward the house. Then he opened the mudroom door and went in. I couldn't go with him; I couldn't go in there again.

Instead, I ran to the side yard where I had previously been running in circles. This time, I lay flat on the ground, pressed my face into the cool grass, and squeezed my eyes shut to block any light from getting through. My mind wanted it to be dark, pitch black—as if not seeing had the power to make none of this be true.

I wanted Marty then, but I didn't know how to get him. At the same time, I wanted to save him from this pain and let him stay blissfully unaware for as long as possible. I lifted my head and briefly opened my eyes just long enough to dial my sister-in-law's phone number.

"Where are you?" I asked.

Andrea could hear the terror in my voice. She said, "What's wrong? Wally and I are at the grocery store."

"I went into Kelsey's house, and she's dead." I shook my head on the ground. "Marty is at work. What should I do?"

She let out a brief cry, but then stopped, knowing she had to act and make decisions. "We'll find Marty and bring him there," she said. "I'll call the girls and tell them to go to the house."

As I hung up my phone, I heard a vehicle pull in. I opened my eyes. It was a sheriff's car. When I saw a familiar face open the car door, I ran to him. The sheriff was a family friend who I'd known for almost forty years.

"Jeff, tell me it isn't true!" I shouted. "Tell me it isn't true."

For a brief, hopeful moment, I thought Jeff might tell me I was wrong.

"Debbie, I'm sorry," he said. "I wish I could."

I shook my head, back and forth. *No, no, no.* Then I ran back to resume my position on the ground; face in the grass, eyes firmly shut, total darkness achieved.

Jeff and the police officer were whispering. I couldn't hear what they were saying, but then Jeff leaned over me and said, "Deb, why don't you get off the ground. We'll get you a chair."

I had no interest in sitting in a chair. "No," I said, without moving.

I heard my nieces enter the yard. They also tried to get me off the ground. I refused, seeing no reason to get up.

It started to rain. Still, I lay there, refusing to move. I thought about how I'd woken up to a warm, sunny day. While Max and I had been walking, enjoying the sun, Kelsey was already lying on her living room floor, having died sometime during the night.

Then it started to rain harder, but being cold and wet didn't matter. My niece held an umbrella over me. I didn't see her or the umbrella, but I heard the raindrops hitting the fabric and noticed only my lower half was getting wet.

"Why don't we put the canopy over her," my niece suggested.

I heard people carrying something and knew one of those large, four legged canopies had been placed over top of me. A vehicle pulled up. I lifted my face to peek. It was Marty stepping out of his truck. I got off the ground and ran into his arms.

He was shaking his head in disbelief. "What happened?" he asked.

I said, "I don't know, but I think she aspirated."

We stood there then, holding each other and crying, not knowing what to do. Then Marty said, "I want to see her." And he pulled away from me and started towards the door.

I was horrified at the idea of him seeing her like that. I yelled, "No! Do not go in there!"

The police helped convince Marty not to go in. I was starting to come back to my senses a bit, and I asked the officer to get Brody's leash and let him into the fenced yard. When he did, I opened the gate and put Brody's leash on. Then we walked up the hill to my brother-in-law's house.

It seemed like there were people everywhere when all I wanted to do was hide. There was my brother-in-law Wally, his wife, Andrea, their daughters Jess and Steph, and Jess's husband, Jay. I sat on their kitchen floor and hugged Brody while people made phone calls. My brother Shawn was going to drive to my mom's to tell her. Louise, Brendan's girlfriend, was going to find him at work. I just wanted to go home.

Soon Jeff came into the house. He called Marty and me into the living room and said, "I have to ask if you want an autopsy?"

I looked at Marty and we both nodded emphatically. "Yes," I said. "We need to know what happened."

"Just so you know," Jeff explained. "It usually takes months to get results from an autopsy."

I crumbled. "Months! I can't wait months to find out what happened."

"I usually encourage people to wait for the final report," Jeff explained. "But the doctor gives me preliminary results about 24 hours after the autopsy. I can share those with you if you want."

There was no question in my mind. "Yes," I said. "Please."

Finally, we got in various cars to go home. I clung to Brody in the backseat, thinking about how much he loved Kelsey and that he'd never get to see her again. There was no way for a dog to understand such a thing. He'd never sit on the couch next to her or play in his backyard. His whole world was about to change.

I thought that being home would somehow make me feel better, but that was a ridiculous notion. More calls were made, and now our house was filled with people. Every time someone new arrived, I hugged them fiercely and cried, "Kelsey is gone! She's gone!"

In my mind, I kept seeing myself reach for the kitchen door. That would always be the last moment I thought Kelsey was alive. Opening the door, finding her, and running from the house was repeating in a continuous loop. It was like sitting in a theater staring at a screen with a horror movie playing, and I couldn't turn it off. If people were watching me, they would've noticed that I'd suddenly start shaking my head in a violent motion. I was trying to stop the movie, turn back time, and not open the door.

Planning a funeral, choosing clothes for Kelsey to wear, and writing a eulogy were all jarring and instant expectations. Finding out what happened to Kelsey was all I could think about. I wanted Marty to message Jeff about the autopsy, but he wanted to stay focused on all the tasks that needed to be done. Finally, I got Jeff's phone number from my sister-in-law. Then I asked him, again, to call me as soon as he got the preliminary results.

A couple of days later, our house was still filled with people when Jeff sent a message with a time he would call. Marty, Brendan, and I found a private place in the basement. The three of us sat on the couch together and waited.

I felt relieved and terribly ill at the same time. All I'd been able to think about since the moment I saw Kelsey was: *What happened?* Now, I was about to find out. When my phone rang, I answered and put it on speaker.

"The doctor told me Kelsey was very sick that night," Jeff explained. "The cause of death was aspiration; vomit went into her lungs, but she vomited because of a severe intestinal blockage."

I wrapped my arms around my stomach and started rocking back and forth. I tried to scream, but no sound came out.

"Thanks for calling, Jeff," Marty said, and then he quickly hung up.

It felt impossible to get the words out, but I had to tell them what felt like a terrible secret. "Kelsey told me something was seriously wrong with her," I said. "She said people would be sorry, and I didn't believe her. This is all my fault." I hadn't told anyone about Kelsey's ominous premonition in the car.

Marty tried to console me, "You're not a doctor. How could you have known? The doctors all told you she was fine."

"Kelsey also said something was wrong with her bowels," I explained. "But she was having so many other symptoms at the same time. We saw the gastro doctor just five days before she died."

"Exactly," Marty said. "Even he didn't know."

There was something else I needed to say, but I was too afraid. I thought if people knew, they'd blame me even more, but I couldn't stand the guilt. I said, "Whenever I drove to Kelsey's house, I was thinking I don't want to do this for the rest of my life."

Brendan leaned over and put his arm around my shoulder. "You wouldn't be human if you didn't feel that way, Mom," he said.

I appreciated his kind words. Still, nothing could be said at that point to convince me her death wasn't my fault. Just having had that negative thought—imagining a life where I didn't have to take care of Kelsey—felt awful and, in retrospect, ominous, as if someone had been listening and granted my wish.

We left the basement to find Brody waiting at the top of the stairs. He greeted us, tail wagging, excited from all the activity. There were people everywhere for him to jump on, steal food from, and get attention from simply by following them around. How lucky he was not to understand that Kelsey was gone, and that everyone was devastated.

Brody was sitting on the couch in our living room just as he would've been doing in his own house. Marty filled a glass with water, sat next to him, and was about to take a sip. Brody leaned over, stuck out his tongue, and drank from the glass like it was the most natural thing for a dog to do. If he could talk, I'm sure he would have said, *Thanks, dude, I was thirsty.* Everyone burst out laughing, including me. Hearing my laughter felt strange and was immediately followed by guilt. I'd broken a rule—parents who have a child who died aren't supposed to laugh, ever again.

A few moments later, Marty noticed he had a voicemail. It was Allison, the wife of Kelsey's softball coach from elementary school. We knew her husband Brian had just died from cancer on the exact same day as Kelsey. After listening to the message, Marty told me, "She said something happened and to give her a call when I have a chance." We were intrigued by this cryptic message. What possibly could have happened that would make her call us now?

I said, "Go in the basement and call her back." The basement was the best place to have a private conversation with a houseful of people.

About five minutes later, Marty came upstairs and motioned for me to follow. "Allison said she was going through Brian's old things in a shed," he explained. "She moved around some boxes and noticed something tucked behind a cinder block. It was an old baseball bat covered with black paint. Only one thing was visible, Kelsey Waffle #5. This moment gave her chills. She asked if we wanted the bat."

Marty and I looked at each other, amazed by this strange coincidence. Allison knew Kelsey had died on the same day as her husband. What were the chances of finding her name in a shed among Brian's old things? He was her coach eighteen years ago. This story gave me an immediate sense of comfort, as if Kelsey were trying to let us know she was okay.

Writing the perfect eulogy when we were in shock, unable to eat, and not sleeping caused an enormous amount of pressure. I was carrying around a notebook and jotting down my thoughts the moment I had them. Otherwise, they would leave me a second later. I sat at the kitchen counter and opened my notebook to share what I'd written with Marty.

"I've been thinking about something," Marty said—but hesitantly, as if he were expecting a negative reaction from me. "How would you feel about putting Marley's ashes in the vault along with the pictures we chose and the letters we wrote to Kelsey?"

Without the slightest hesitation, I said, "I love that idea." It didn't require any thought. This was perfect. I was grateful that Marty had thought of this before it was too late.

Marley had died four years ago, but his ashes were still in a cabinet. We had talked about getting permission to spread his ashes at our previous home where Cocoa and Hershey were buried. Another idea had been to put them under his favorite tree in our backyard. Kelsey was the main reason we'd never made a final decision. Because she was still traumatized by his death, I had avoided bringing it up. Now we knew: His ashes belonged in the vault with her.

"I've been thinking about something too," I told Marty. "Before we even got Brody, Kelsey and I talked about him becoming a therapy dog. This was a goal she had for the two of them. We had another conversation about this recently when she was having such an awful summer. I feel like I need Brody to become a therapy dog because it's what Kelsey wanted."

"She would love that," Marty said. "We'll have to make sure that happens and share this with everyone in her eulogy."

The eulogy had three parts. First, Marty read a letter written by Brendan to his sister. It said he knew Kelsey had been restricted by her health, and that because she'd been strong for so long, she had motivated him to be the best he could be. "I wanted to make you proud," he wrote. "You were an inspiration to me." He signed it, "Until we meet again, your little brother, Brendan."

Then Marty read a letter to Kelsey telling her all the things we wished we'd told her before she died. We knew that she had felt misunderstood by everyone in her life; that, because people had not seen an obvious cause for her pain, they'd often lacked compassion for her. This had made her feel alone. When Marty or I dealt with even a brief illness or injury, we'd be miserable and wonder how Kelsey lived like this all the time. Now, we said we wished we had told her more often how much we admired her strength to live with chronic pain.

Marty also assured Kelsey that her life story hadn't ended, because Brody would become a therapy dog in her memory. We would make sure that the people Brody visited would know her story, that Brody was there because of her.

The third letter was from Kelsey to the family. Marty and I imagined what we thought Kelsey would want to say to her grandparents, Brendan, Louise, and of course Marley and Brody. She would tell Louise how much she appreciated that Louise always took time to talk to and listen to her; she'd tell Brody how he gave her a purpose and was the highlight of her day.

Somehow, Marty found the strength to get up there and read these letters out loud. He said, "Kelsey deserves this eulogy. And it needs to be given by me."

Part II

Chapter Fifteen

On Wednesday night at 6:00, exactly one week after Kelsey died, Brody and I walked into a dog agility class. I didn't want to be there, but Kelsey and I had signed up for this class months ago.

The Friday after I'd found Kelsey, I called the place where the class was being held. "My daughter just died," I told the person who had the misfortune of answering the phone that morning. "I'd like to cancel."

The girl said, "Of course. I'm sorry for your loss."

Yet all weekend I couldn't stop thinking about the class. I knew how excited Kelsey had been for Brody to have this experience. I also couldn't stop thinking about all the memoirs I'd shared with Kelsey where eventually, something good had come from something bad. Now, I wondered if I was strong enough to emulate all the people I'd read about.

The following Monday, I called the place back. "Would it be okay if Brody and I rejoined the class?" I asked.

"No problem," she said. "I'll put you two back on the list."

The class was held in a gym-like space, because the room had to accommodate a 12-foot-long balance beam with 12-foot ramps on each end, hurdles made from PC piping, a seesaw, a 6-foot-tall A-frame ramp, weaving poles, and an expandable dog tunnel. Sets of chairs were spread out along the sides of the room. I chose a seat, and Brody put his head in my lap, wide-eyed and panting. New environments make him nervous. By the time class was ready to start, there were a total of six dogs.

Michelle, the instructor, said, "Let's go around the room and introduce everyone."

When it was my turn, I said, "My name is Debbie Waffle, and this is my golden retriever Brody."

It was the only thing to say; there was no way I could tell them, "This is my daughter's dog; she died last week." It took every ounce of strength I had not to start weeping. I didn't want the people to know what happened and feel sorry for me. I reminded myself we were there for two reasons: because this class had been important to Kelsey, and because this would help Brody become a therapy dog. I had no idea what skills were on the therapy dog test, but training of any kind, including agility, would help Brody gain confidence in himself and me as his partner.

Michelle pulled out a 3-foot-wide circle with a ball in the middle that raised it off the floor at an angle. She said, "This is called a wobble board. Your dog needs to walk across the circle and not care when one side falls to the ground."

I watched a couple of dogs successfully walk across the board, unfazed by its see-saw movement. When it was our turn, I put a few treats in a line on the board. Brody stepped on the board confidently, but the moment it wobbled, he leaped off as if it were alive.

Michelle said, "Try again."

This time when I put the treats down, Brody stretched out his neck and walked around the circle eating them without stepping on the board. Everyone in the class smiled, including me.

Next, Michelle showed us a balance beam that was a foot wide and only a few inches off the ground. "Put treats along the board so your dog will walk across it," she explained, while demonstrating with a border collie who pranced across the beam effortlessly.

When I tried to get Brody to step on the board using treats, he again just ate them while walking alongside the beam. This was much easier than the wobble board because he didn't even need to stretch out his neck. We tried a few more times, but he refused to step on the beam. "Don't worry," Michelle allowed. "Sometimes it takes them a few classes to get it."

By the time we left, Brody had gotten dozens of treats without doing anything. I felt a little discouraged, but reminded myself that Brody had had fun, which would have made Kelsey happy. That's what mattered most.

*　　*　　*

The next day, I proceeded to Kelsey's as usual, moving boxes and storage bins in tow. I'm not sure why I'd immediately felt the need to empty her house. I'd been going there almost every day—maybe because going there was what I was used to doing. Holding her belongings made me feel closer to her. And every time I walked in, it helped remind me that she wasn't there. I'd walk up to the couch, run my hands along the place she always sat, and cry out, "I'm sorry! Please forgive me."

Marty had one request. "I don't want to walk in and feel like it isn't Kelsey's house," he said. "I'm not ready for that." So, I emptied closets, drawers, and cabinets, but left out most of the items you could see.

I'd load up my car and make sure there was enough time to put everything in the attic before Marty got home from work. I didn't want him to see all her things being carried through our house because Kelsey didn't need them anymore. It was strange, though. Before, going to Kelsey's house had made me angry. Now I didn't know how to stop.

I started seeing a counselor, something I should've done a long time before. I told her, "I find it helps to keep really busy."

She said, "Well that's good."

But then I elaborated. "I'd call it more of a manic busyness. I need to be in constant motion, or my only thoughts are about how Kelsey died. The worst thing is to be still. Falling asleep is only possible when I'm totally exhausted."

"Oh, that's not good," she said, sounding a bit more concerned. "There's something for us to work on."

I also told her that the car was my crying place. Probably because if you're driving, you must be still. I'm usually alone in the car, so I don't have to pretend I'm okay. I look over at the passenger seat and Kelsey isn't there. In her place is a full-size box of tissues.

My mom has called many times while I'm driving. I answer using the car speaker. As soon as I say "Hello," she notices the quiver in my voice and asks, "Are you crying in the car again?"

I remind her, "The car is my crying place." She finds this concerning because she doesn't think crying and driving go well together. "No need to worry," I say with confidence. "I've gotten very good at it."

I also shared with Marty how hard it was for me to be in the car. "Do you want to get a new one?" he asked. I said no, then explained to him that the car was where Kelsey and I had spent much of our time together, where we'd had many conversations.

She was 26 when she'd announced from the passenger seat, "We all would've been better off if I'd never been born."

At first, I just sat there quietly, not sure how to respond. I was thinking, *What a sad thing to think, feel, and say*, but I also understood exactly why Kelsey felt this way. Instead of validating her feelings and having a discussion, I'd said, "Don't talk like that," and changed the subject. Now, I wish I'd said more. Much of our lives as a family had been affected by her chronic illness. She was feeling guilty about how her symptoms had a negative impact on everyone. I wish I had told her that none of this was her fault, and that she didn't choose to be sick.

As our attic became filled with her belongings, I thought it would be helpful to surround Marty and me with reminders of Kelsey. Not that we needed reminders, but I thought we'd find it comforting. I put pictures of her all over the house. She had bought some household decorations after moving in, which I now put on our shelves. I took a picture of how Kelsey had decorated her kitchen windowsill and then replicated it. Above our kitchen sink, I put her ceramic letter K, two flowered vases, the word love written in cursive, and a picture of her and Marty taken at a concert. When I finished redecorating our home, Kelsey's beautiful face and belongings were everywhere we turned.

"This is too much for me," Marty said.

I'd been thinking the same thing but thought maybe I deserved to suffer. At 11:00 PM, I started frantically running around the house removing everything I'd done.

Marty said, "I didn't mean you had to do it right now."

I was crazed and angry as I tossed everything back into boxes, not at Marty, but at myself for thinking this was a good idea. And because my daughter no longer needed all these items she had once owned and cherished.

When everything was gone, Marty said, "Keep out the pictures of Kelsey and Brody at Wintergreen Park."

I had two photos in a hinged frame from that October day when Kelsey and I walked along the gorge with Brody. In the picture on the left, Kelsey is walking on the trail with 8-month-old Brody by her side. In the picture on the right, she's kneeling next to him on the observation deck that overlooks the waterfall. I constantly pass by these pictures in my kitchen and remember that day fondly. Kelsey felt good; she's wearing a green T-shirt and smiling.

Just two weeks before she died, I'd dropped Kelsey off for an appointment with her general practitioner, and Brody and I walked on the bike path while we waited. When she was done, we went to my house, just five minutes down the road. Marty showed Kelsey some videos he'd made using an App on his phone.

Kelsey said, "Dad, those videos are hysterical. How do you do that?"

"You choose a picture and a song," Marty explained. "Then the App makes it look like the person is singing. Ready?" Kelsey was standing in front of our refrigerator when Marty took her picture. She just happened to be wearing the same green T-shirt from that day at Wintergreen Park.

Then Marty pulled the App up on his phone and said, "Pick a song."

The three of us watched the video. It looked like Kelsey was singing the song. Now, late at night, when I'm missing her, I look over at the refrigerator and see her standing there wearing her green T-shirt. It was the last time she was at our house.

Chapter Sixteen

Brody and I continued our agility class training. Michelle set up hurdles and weaving poles. If I threw a treat over a hurdle and said, "Jump," Brody leaped over the hurdle from a standstill, looking more like a deer than a dog, which made everyone laugh. When I held a treat in a closed fist, Brody smelled it and followed my hand as he weaved between poles, getting the reward only when he finished.

Part of the course included a six-foot-tall A-frame ramp. It went up at a steep angle, and once the dog reached the top, it suddenly veered back to the floor. This seemed like Brody's favorite thing to do, because he ran up and down the ramp exuberantly without even needing a treat.

Michelle set up a bicycle tire that hung from a metal frame. At first, Brody resisted jumping through the tire. She asked, "What kind of treats are you using?"

I said, "Just little training treats I bought at the pet store."

"Did anyone bring hot dogs?" Michelle asked the group.

Someone handed me cut up pieces of hot dogs from their treat pouch. I tossed them into the hole of the tire and Brody eagerly jumped through. Michelle said, "You need to give him a better reward."

The next week I brought chunks of hot dogs instead of training treats. Now Brody would do just about anything I asked. If I threw a few pieces of hot dogs into the long, dark tunnel, he hesitated, but then ran through the tunnel when I called his name from the other end.

Brody's biggest challenge was the balance beam. Instead of being inches from the floor as it was the first night, it was now three feet off the ground. First Brody had to go up a 12-foot ramp. Then there was a flat 12-foot beam to walk across that was only a foot wide, followed by another ramp that brought him safely back to the floor. Getting on the beam was the hardest part, but a trail of hot dogs certainly helped. Once Brody made the decision to step on the beam, he realized that walking across it wasn't that bad. It was that first step that was always the hardest.

I say Brody would do almost anything for hot dogs, but he still refused to step on the wobble board or walk across a seesaw. At first, the seesaw looked just like any other ramp, so he got on without issue and took a few steps. Towards the middle, his weight would shift the plank, causing it to fall to the floor. Every time this happened, Brody jumped off the seesaw like there'd been an earthquake. He'd look at me, confused, like, *Didn't you feel that?* Lesson learned: Brody doesn't like things that move suddenly beneath his feet. I can't say I blame him.

On the last night of class, Michelle set up a course for everyone to run through and get timed, just for fun. We lucked out that she didn't include the wobble board or the seesaw. When it was Brody's turn, he jumped over hurdles, went up and down the A-frame, weaved between poles, jumped through the tire, raced through the tunnel, and even walked across the balance beam. After the beam, all he had to do was sit for three seconds and then the timer stopped. Brody completed the course in 2 minutes and 37 seconds—a good time. As I walked back to my chair so the next dog could go, thinking Brody was just behind me, everyone started laughing. I turned around to see why, and there was Brody back on the balance beam.

Michelle said, "Just keep going."

As I did, Brody walked across the beam, this time without praise or treats. At the end, out of six dogs, his time put him in second place. The progress Brody made from the first class to the last was inspiring. I was proud of him; also terribly sad that Kelsey wasn't there to watch.

Every day I found it necessary to feel connected to Kelsey in some way. Agility classes and spending time with Brody helped accomplish this. Part of my manic busyness included making new photo albums that represented Kelsey's life. I sorted her sentimental belongings into categories and bought a hope chest to store them in. That way I could walk by the chest and know all her things were close by.

I'd also been looking forward to seeing the baseball bat that Allison found. One evening, Marty and I drove to her house with an apple pie. She retold the story of how the bat was in Brian's shed and how surprised she was when she saw Kelsey's name. Kelsey having died on the same day as her husband was such a strange coincidence. Once I held the bat in my hands, I could tell the other players had signed it, but just as Allison had described, now it was all black with only one name showing—Kelsey Waffle #5, written in her handwriting. I showed Allison a picture I found of eleven-year-old Kelsey in her softball uniform with Brian standing next to the team. That night, we brought the bat home, and I put it in the hope chest.

Allison had shared information about Kelsey because she thought it was important. She'd contacted us immediately, even though her husband had just died. This made me realize I'd made a mistake and needed to talk to someone else I knew—but I didn't have her phone number, and at the time wasn't a part of any social media.

In December of 2021, I'd been at a craft fair in a mall filled with holiday shoppers. My jewelry was displayed in white trays, and necklaces hung from hooks attached to picture frames. A young girl in a wheelchair stopped at my table with a woman who was helping her.

The girl was moving back and forth trying to see all the pendants, and she kept saying, "She loves purple." I had many different purple stones wrapped in silver wire, strung on cord necklaces. The stones varied in shades of purple, had unique markings, and may have been round or oval shaped. She chose one and started bringing it to me.

But on her way, she spotted another purple stone and said, "I think I like this one better." Then she handed me the pendant.

The woman with the girl said, "There's another purple stone over here."

"Wait," the girl told me as I was wrapping tissue paper around the necklace she'd chosen. "I'm sorry I keep changing my mind."

I said, "No worries. You can change your mind as often as you like."

The girl made a final decision and handed me a credit card. When I was putting the pendant in a box, she proudly announced, "I've beaten cancer three times."

"Congratulations," I said. "That's wonderful news." Then I gave her a little silver bag with her purchase inside.

"Are you on Facebook?" the woman asked. "Alyssa has a lot of followers."

"Sorry, I'm not," I answered.

I thanked them, and we said goodbye. As I watched them leave, I thought about the woman calling the girl Alyssa. Years before, I had known a family with a daughter named Alyssa who had leukemia. Now, since she'd paid with a credit card, I thought maybe the card reader would show me her last name. It worked. The girl who bought the pendant used to be my neighbor on Brower Road. I knew her mom, Karen, and the rest of her family.

That day at the mall, it had probably been eight years since we'd last seen each other. Kelsey had babysat Alyssa and her younger sister a couple of times. Alyssa's brother and Brendan used to play together. Several times, Karen had watched Brendan after school when Kelsey had appointments. Both our families had left Brower Road and now lived in different towns.

Just three weeks after the craft fair, Alyssa died. She was only 23. When I heard what happened, I couldn't believe it. The pendant was a Christmas present, and she died on December 30th. I had no idea who the necklace was for, or who in Alyssa's life loved purple. My first thought after I'd heard this was that I should call Karen. She would want to know how Alyssa had chosen the stone with such care, how excited she was about this gift. But then I'd decided to wait and let some time go by. I felt uncomfortable, and wondered, *What do you say to someone whose daughter just died?*

As more and more time passed, I thought about Karen, Alyssa, and their family a lot, but I kept avoiding making that call. I never could've imagined that nine months later, I'd be the one whose daughter died. If someone had information about Kelsey, I'd want them to share it with me—as Allison had with the baseball bat.

Karen had remarried. I knew her husband and his last name. For over an hour, I did searches trying to find her phone number. Many numbers I called were out of service. Some I dialed went to voicemails I knew were wrong. I spoke to a few people who had no idea who Karen was.

Finally, I heard a voice I recognized, and knew immediately it was Karen's husband. I said, "I'm so happy I found you. This is Debbie Waffle. I've been trying to find Karen's phone number. Is she there?"

Her husband said, "She's right here." Then I heard him say, "It's Debbie Waffle," as he handed Karen the phone.

"I've been wanting to call and ask you a question," I explained. "Did Alyssa give you a purple stone for Christmas?"

Karen paused. I could tell she was confused. "Yes," she answered hesitantly.

I said, "Alyssa bought the pendant from me at a craft fair."

She started to cry and then told me a story:

"The cancer had spread to Alyssa's brain, and she was having trouble remembering things. On Christmas morning, Alyssa was terribly upset because she had a special present for me but couldn't remember where she put it. All day she kept talking about the missing gift. The woman at the mall with her that day was a nurse who had become a close friend as she cared for Alyssa. The day of the wake, I was at the funeral home when she walked in saying, I found it, I found it! Then she handed me the purple stone, Alyssa's last gift to me. The pendant was found while Alyssa's room was being cleaned. I felt relieved when the gift was finally in my hand. Ever since that day, I've kept the stone in my pocket and have carried it with me everywhere. I knew it was special for some reason, and now I know why. Our girls brought us together."

We talked about the anguish of missing our daughters and knowing it would always be this way. What I didn't know then was that grieving people have a knack for finding each other. Once people know you're suffering from this type of loss, other grievers are out there just waiting to share their stories.

*　　*　　*

"I can't sleep," I told a doctor, maybe in her 40's. "When I wake up at 2:00 or 3:00 in the morning, all I can think about is that Kelsey's gone, and I can't get her back. I lie there for hours. Falling back to sleep just isn't possible."

The doctor sat across from me in the exam room, not speaking, not moving. I've been in this situation enough to recognize this abnormal behavior. I expected her to write me a script and promptly run out the door. Instead, she said, "My son died." The doctor then told me her own grief story.

"If you'd like," she said, when she'd finished, "you could give me a piece of Kelsey's clothing and I'll make it into a pillow. It's something I like to do for people."

I said, "I'd like that very much."

As soon as I got home, I went to the attic where much of Kelsey's clothing was still stored in bins. Instead of choosing something recent, I thought about what Kelsey loved most—hoodies. As a middle school student, she'd lived in hoodies that had colorful patterns and were considered "skate hoodies" even though she wasn't a skateboarder. I chose a sweatshirt that was her favorite brand and had a crisscross pattern in shades of red and tan. Kelsey had worn this hoodie on an almost weekly basis when she was in eighth grade. The pillow turned out perfectly, with real pockets and a zipper down the center, just like the original hoodie. I loved it and understood this was the doctor's way of offering a bit of comfort to those who were grieving, as she was.

Just thirteen days before Kelsey died, I had brought her to her general practitioner's office. She'd had monthly appointments there, because some of her medications were controlled substances. Brody and I first walked on a nearby bike path and then continued walking around the doctor's parking lot while we waited for Kelsey.

A husband and wife came up to us. The woman said, "I love his red coloring. I'm hoping to get a golden retriever with that color. Where did he come from?"

Just like Kelsey, I reveled in getting compliments about Brody. "I have the breeder's information at home," I told them. "If you want to exchange phone numbers, I'll send it to you. The breeder has a couple of litters each year."

While we were talking, Kelsey came out and joined our conversation. "He is a wonderful dog," she told them. Then she laughed out loud as she recalled a recent event. "Brody is usually very good about leaving my food alone. But one night he snatched a fry right off my plate. I was surprised and firmly told him No! Then he dropped the fry on the floor right in front of me."

The couple were impressed. "How did you teach him to do that?" the woman asked.

Kelsey said, "I didn't. He's just smart."

Later, I texted Robin, the woman, the breeder's information. After Kelsey died, Robin contacted me. I wasn't going to mention what happened. This woman and I had simply met in a parking lot. But then she said, "How is your daughter doing?"

What could I do other than tell her the truth?

She expressed heartfelt sympathy, adding that Kelsey had "seemed full of life, especially with Brody by her side." She paused, then said, "I understand. We lost a grandson when he was only five years old. He had a congenital birth defect that the doctors never caught. It left us in shock, pain, and denial for months. Then came the tears and the healing. It is a long process." As always, there was that surprise, and then relief, of meeting someone who understood.

For my first Christmas without Kelsey, Marty gave me a trip to Ireland! Patty and I would ride horses for a week, from a farmhouse in Whitegate to the Cliffs of Moher. When we arrived, we met the six other women we'd be riding with, four from Ohio, one from California, and another from Germany.

After the first couple of days, Patty and I lay down in our beds after riding our horses for about fourteen miles. We had already turned out the lights, exhausted, and were just starting to fall asleep. I'm not sure why, but as I lay there, a question came to mind. I said to Patty, "What do you think I should say if someone asks me if I have children?" This was my first experience meeting people who had no idea my daughter had died. We then discussed different ways to answer this question.

Less than twelve hours later, I was sitting on my horse when Holly, the rider behind me, asked, "Deb, do you have any children?"

Because we were in a line, she couldn't see the shocked expression on my face. I was glad that Patty and I had just talked about this exact situation. "I have a son and a daughter," I told Holly. "But my daughter, Kelsey, recently passed away. She was only 29."

I appreciated that instead of just spouting some cliché like "I'm sorry for your loss" and then changing the subject, Holly asked me questions about Kelsey. It felt good to talk about her. During the rest of our time together, Holly and I had many similar conversations. She was an easy person to talk to.

"I had a friend who passed away," Holly shared with me. "Then my mother died just a few days later." I also learned that at the age of 47, Holly's sister died from cancer. Here was a person who knew a lot about grief.

When I returned home, I sent Holly some gifts and she wrote me a letter. In the letter she told me I was brave, and that my beautiful, timely gifts were a healing balm to a wound she didn't realize she was still carrying. Her words were a reminder that when someone is grieving, it's the little things we do for them that matter. Sometimes small gestures can have big results.

A few weeks later, I was talking to a friend I hadn't seen in a long time. Tracy had lived across the street from Marty and me at our first home when Kelsey was little. She had watched Kelsey grow up on our little cul-de-sac with only four houses; our kids played outside together and were always riding their bikes around the circular road. Tracy and her children came to all of Kelsey's birthday parties. Every year we went trick-or-treating with them, including that Halloween when Kelsey was a fish tank.

We were just standing there talking about Kelsey and sharing memories. Another person I didn't even know had overheard our conversation. She said, "My brother died a long time ago. This morning, I woke up and felt out of sorts because I couldn't stop thinking about him. Listening to your story has reminded me that I'm not alone."

Suddenly, everywhere I turned there were grieving people. They'd always been there, of course, but now they seemed to recognize that I was one of them. Without knowing it, I'd joined a club no one wants to be a part of. As an elementary school teacher, if I wanted to have a conversation about classroom behavior, I'd talk to another teacher. If Marty wanted to have a conversation about computers, he wouldn't have this conversation with me. He would discuss technical problems with a person proficient in technology. So, it makes sense that grieving people find it easier to talk to others who are grieving. And, as with the girl whose brother died, they all made me feel less lonely.

Chapter Seventeen

I try to imagine what it would be like to die at 29. At that age, Marty and I were living in our first home and had been married for seven years. We were the parents of a two-year-old, and I was pregnant. My father was still alive. Remembering that time makes me realize how young Kelsey was. At 29, it felt like my life was just beginning. Hers was ending.

A part of me will always be stuck in that moment—I get out of the car, I enter the mudroom, I get the keys back out of my purse, I open the kitchen door. This is the great divide that created a Before and an After. When I see Before pictures of myself, this person looks like a stranger. She was Kelsey's mom. Of course I'll always be Kelsey's mother, but I feel disconnected from this person, because she no longer exists. The After pictures of myself also feel like someone I don't know.

She is living in a world where her daughter is missing. I'm still trying to figure out who she is.

Every night since September 28th, I've closed my eyes and prayed to see Kelsey in a dream. I was jealous when Marty woke up on two occasions and told me he saw her. He couldn't remember any words being spoken, just that she was wearing a dress.

Then one night, in a dream, I found myself standing in a laundromat. When I looked out the window, I knew I was in Fonda, the town where Kelsey had lived. I noticed her red car was parked out front. The door to the laundromat opened, and Kelsey walked in. We stood there for a moment staring at each other. She looked much younger, as she did in middle school, and she was wearing black athletic shorts. Her phone rang, and she answered it without speaking. Then she looked at me and said, "I have to go." Even though her car was parked outside, she ran down the sidewalk. I opened the door and looked in the direction Kelsey ran, but she was gone. Even though this dream doesn't make any sense, I woke up feeling like I saw her.

I was curious, and asked Patty, "Is there a laundromat in Fonda?"

"There used to be," she answered. "But it isn't there anymore." After I told her about the dream, she said, "When God calls, you listen."

This made me laugh. I'm not sure why I didn't tell Marty about the dream. I think sometimes I simply believe that not talking about Kelsey might lessen his pain. We own a building in Fonda that Marty and I talked about selling if it didn't get leased soon. One day Marty came home from work and said, "What if we turn the building into a laundromat?"

I looked at Marty wide-eyed and stunned. I couldn't believe he was asking me this question. Even though this was an unbelievable coincidence, I said, "I don't think that's a good idea." My retired self has no interest in managing a laundromat. Instead of thinking my dream about Kelsey was some kind of endorsement, I jokingly thought it was more of a warning.

After Kelsey moved out, I'd get in bed at night and check my phone to see if she'd messaged me. I'd read a book while waiting to get sleepy, but if I didn't fall asleep soon, I'd check my phone one more time before I closed my eyes. The moment I awoke, I'd reach over and feel around on the nightstand. With eyes barely open, I'd see if she'd tried to contact me during the night. The urge to do these things is still there.

Kelsey's phone sits on a charger in her old bedroom. I think it will stay there indefinitely. For a while, occasionally I'd pick it up and see more than fifty messages from our twelve-person family group chat. It bothered me that these messages were still coming to her phone, but I didn't know how to make them stop.

I told Patty, and she said, "You have to do this on her phone," but she used my phone to show me. She touched the picture at the top of the group chat and a list of all twelve people popped up on the screen. Then she scrolled to the bottom and said, "Choose to leave this conversation."

A few days later, I happened to be in Kelsey's room, where I now store things, when I heard a message come through. My sister had just sent a picture of her three children. I followed Patty's directions to leave the conversation, but it didn't make me feel better, as I had thought it would. Now every time I get a message from the group, it says eleven instead of twelve.

There are constant blaring reminders shouting at me every day—Kelsey is gone. The most obvious is I don't have to take care of her anymore. Taking care of Kelsey had consumed so much of my time. I had imagined how much better my life would be if I didn't have to do this. But in my scenario, Kelsey was simply taking care of *herself*—not dead.

Then there are less blatant reminders that can be just as painful. My mom made an appointment with a new dentist in a town she was unfamiliar with. Even though I didn't want to go there when I realized it was Kelsey's dentist, I volunteered to drive her. We'd be repeating the same day I'd had with Kelsey many times—park the car, walk Brody, wait for my phone to ring. As Brody and I walked the village streets, all I could think about was the phone in my pocket. Every time I'd been here before, it would ring and be Kelsey.

She'd say, "Mom, I'm done."

I'd estimate how far away we were and tell her, "We'll be back as soon as we can."

Waiting for my phone to ring now was agonizing and made my chest physically hurt. When it finally rang, it startled me, as if I'd been in a trance. The sound brought me back to the present. I reached for my phone.

At that moment, I imagined hearing Kelsey's voice. But of course, it wasn't Kelsey, it was my mom saying, "I'm done."

I raced to the parking lot with Brody. I needed to get away from here as soon as possible. When I dropped my mom off at her house, it felt like I could breathe again.

My morning routine had been to feed Max, let him out, make a cup of coffee, then go to my jewelry desk. Over the months, Marty must have noticed that I wasn't going to my jewelry desk the way I used to. He asked me several times, "Why don't you make your jewelry anymore?"

Each time he asked, I said, "I'm not sure. Making jewelry just doesn't feel right." I wasn't being honest. There was a reason I'd stopped, but I didn't want to say it.

Marty kept asking, and one day I told him the truth. "If I hadn't been working that day trying to sell my jewelry, I would've gone to see Kelsey because she was in so much pain."

Following this logic, my jewelry could be the reason Kelsey died. I've gone to my jewelry desk a few times to see if I still felt any of my previous joy and creativity. Before, when I'd looked at my stones and beads, I'd get a vision of what I wanted them to become. Now, my mind goes blank. I don't see anything, and I walk away feeling sad.

I mentioned this to my counselor. She reminded me that Kelsey had lived in pain, and there was no way for me to have known that this time would be different. Most nights, when I went to sleep, I knew Kelsey would be awake struggling with one or more of her symptoms, but the next day she was always there. When I opened the kitchen door, I had every reason to believe I'd find Kelsey asleep on the couch. On an intellectual level, I understand and agree with this reasoning. But my emotional side intervenes and takes over.

The counselor also validated my feelings. "What you've been through will change you," she said. "It's okay if you don't want to make jewelry now. Maybe someday you'll feel differently." I'm quite sure I'll never be able to separate making jewelry from Kelsey dying. In my mind they will always be connected.

I'd been going back and forth trying to decide if this was a good idea or not. A part of me wanted so badly to see Kelsey walking and smiling, to hear her voice, while at the same time, part of me was terrified to see her alive. One day I couldn't stand the torment any longer. I sat on the couch and turned on the television. Brody jumped up beside me as he always does. This was usually the perfect opportunity for him to be petted nonstop with my free left hand. He had no idea how different this time was going to be when I pressed Play on the DVD player.

For hours, I watched Kelsey wake up on Christmas mornings, celebrate birthdays, hunt for Easter eggs, welcome home her new brother, and visit the pumpkin patch. This whole time I howled with a deep guttural sound I'd never heard coming from myself before. The noise I made was scary.

Almost immediately, Brody left my side to go hide in his crate, something he'd never done before. I knew how painful it would be to see Kelsey move on screen as a living person, but I hadn't anticipated how difficult it would be to see myself. During those early years, I'm carefree and happy. I'd always wanted to be a mom, and now I had everything I'd ever wanted. I watched my younger self and wanted to shout at her—you have no idea what is coming! When I first decided to watch the DVDs, I'd planned on watching them all, but the misery I felt was exhausting. I also was worried about Brody.

Even when I stood in front of the crate's open door, Brody just lay there looking at me, as if he were afraid to come out. I sat on the floor and held out my arms. "It's okay," I told him.

Brody ran to me and stayed in my lap for several minutes. Then I said, "Let's go for a walk." We both needed a distraction and some fresh air.

I had purposely watched the DVDs when Marty was out of town. There was no need for him to witness the torture I chose to inflict upon myself. But he was home the night I sat down and took a sip from a flavored water bottle. I must've swallowed wrong, because afterwards, I couldn't breathe for a moment, and it felt like I was choking. Then my gag reflex caused the water to fly out of my mouth. For the next five minutes, I couldn't stop coughing. It felt like some liquid had gone into my lungs.

Marty was downstairs when this happened. He came upstairs and found me crying hysterically. "What's wrong?" he asked.

I tried to speak, but the words came out garbled between gasps of air.

Marty said, "I can't understand you."

Eventually I calmed down enough to explain. My hysterics had nothing to do with what had happened to me. They were because I kept imagining how scared Kelsey must have been when she knew she was dying.

I'll never be able to close my eyes at night and think, *Today was a great day*. People might say it's too soon, that I shouldn't think like that, but I disagree. The happiness I feel during occasions with family and friends can never be 100 percent. No matter how much time passes, a part of me will always be allocated to feeling sad. The key is learning how to live with a never-ending sadness.

For most of Kelsey's life, I put her first, as mothers are supposed to with their children; I showed her unconditional love. But in the end, I disappointed her, even as *she* showed *me* that love. For a long time after she died, I wanted to tell her that this was my biggest regret; that even though I was the mother she needed for most of her life, I failed and disappointed her at the end. "I should have listened when you told me something was seriously wrong," I wanted to tell her. "When you answered your phone at 8:37 and said you were in pain, I should have driven to your house instead of going to sleep while you were dying. I shouldn't have renovated the house. Then you wouldn't have been alone and maybe I could have saved you."

I wanted to say to her, "When I ask myself why you didn't tell me to come over, take you to the emergency room, call 911… I know the answer. Everyone, including myself, taught you to stop asking for help." I wanted to tell her I'm sorry.

But I couldn't, and in the months after Kelsey died, this was all I could think about. My energy was consumed by wishing I could tell her those things. Even with all her medical problems, it had never occurred to me that Kelsey could die from her symptoms. I'm sure it hadn't occurred to her doctors either, who never in any way indicated that her symptoms were serious or life-threatening.

She left unexpectedly; I hadn't gotten to say goodbye. This made me envious of parents who did get to say goodbye to their child. I knew this was selfish, because it meant that the child probably knew they were dying. But if I'd had the chance to tell Kelsey my thoughts and feelings, I thought, maybe it would be possible to imagine a meaningful future without her. Instead, I was spending each day trying to figure out how I could have saved her.

In an airport gift shop, I was wandering around trying to pass the time. There was a book title that caught my attention: *Power Prayers to Grow Your Faith*. I'm not one to typically read religious books, but when I saw the book was only $5.99, I bought it.

One morning, I was struggling even more than usual with overwhelming guilt. I couldn't stop crying and asking myself if Kelsey would forgive my behavior. It seemed wrong and unnatural for a daughter to be the one giving unconditional love to her mother. I was still crying when I opened this book to get my mind on something else.

There was a brief introduction about faith, the assurance about what we do not see. Then I turned the page and saw "Chapter 1—The Power of Unconditional Love." I stared at the page and kept repeating these words. At that moment, I knew the answer to my question: Kelsey would forgive me. She knew how much I loved her.

The real problem was how to forgive myself.

Chapter Eighteen

When Kelsey and I were leaving her house and couldn't take Brody with us, we had always put him in his dog crate. He didn't seem to mind, because this is what we'd done since he was a puppy. I'd toss in a few treats, close the door, and say, "Okay." Brody would turn in circles, looking for the treats while I quietly left the house. Inside the crate was his blanket and toys to play with until our return.

I continued doing this when Brody came to live with us. But during the night, he was free to roam around. He never bothered with anything, and in the morning, I usually found him curled up on the couch we put in the living room just for him. One day when I left, I decided not to put him in his crate.

Five hours later, I walked in the house and said, "Hello guys," meaning of course Max and Brody.

Max was standing there with my slippers in his mouth like he always does, but Brody was nowhere in sight.

This time I called his name. "Brody?"

As I walked around looking for him, I started to get worried. "Brody!" I said again, much louder.

When I turned the corner into Brendan's former bedroom, I found Brody lying in his crate with the door wide open. He had a look on his face that said you forgot to put me in here. Even though I was calling his name, Brody didn't even stand up until he saw me. I laughed as he ran into my arms for a big hug. With his head resting on my shoulder, I thought, what would I do without you?

Brody became my life preserver. Sometimes I felt this was a lot of pressure to put on the little guy. My goal was for him to take the therapy dog test in the spring, but I thought this was probably too soon. He still had a lot of puppy behaviors—jumping on people or peeing if he got too excited. In the backyard, he'd start running in circles for no apparent reason. I loved his puppy-like ways and didn't want to make him grow up too fast.

In my area, I couldn't find specific classes designed for dogs to become therapy dogs, but when I asked a trainer what the best class was to help prepare for the test, she said Canine Good Citizen. Even though this class was offered close to home, I signed up to take it at a place in Albany. This was an hour's drive, but only five minutes from Brendan's apartment. Brendan and Louise, now his fiancée, were going to take care of Brody while Marty and I went to Florida for two weeks. They adored Brody, and he loved them dearly, but the thought of leaving him terrified me. My plan was to take Brody to their apartment and spend time there, so that when we left for Florida, he'd be more comfortable.

I drove to Brendan's after the first class. Their apartment was on the sixth floor, and Brody had never been on an elevator before. Therapy dogs need to get on and off elevators all the time. This was the perfect opportunity for him to learn this skill.

When the doors opened, Brody jumped back, surprised by their movement. I threw pieces of hot dog on the elevator floor and said, "Go get it!"

Brody wasn't about to step over the threshold into this strange looking room. I threw in more hot dogs and then stepped into the elevator without him. I said, "Brody come," while keeping the doors open. Brody didn't want to be left behind. He leaped over the crack and eagerly ate the hot dogs. When the elevator started to move, he flattened himself to the floor like he was holding on during an amusement park ride.

The following week, he didn't want to get on the elevator, but it took a little less convincing. He was still scared when the elevator moved, which reminded me of the wobble board and the seesaw from his agility training.

After each class, Brendan and Louise had dinner waiting for me. Their kitchen table had a glass top, which Brody had never seen before. While we ate, he sat underneath the table and gazed up at us through the glass. It was funny to look down at your plate and see his adorable face staring back at you.

By the time we dropped Brody off to leave for Florida, he was used to the apartment and a pro at getting on the elevator. Now, when the elevator moved, he didn't even seem to notice. Still, saying goodbye to him was hard. I kept telling myself it was good for us to have some time apart. We were clearly becoming codependent, or at least I was. I had a lost feeling whenever I wasn't with him.

I missed Brody terribly while we were away. It helped when Brendan and Louise sent pictures of him lounging with them on the couch. While walking in a nearby park, Louise told me they met a young girl with a disability who wanted to pet Brody. She said Brody was gentle, as if he knew not to be his usual rambunctious self with her. When it was time to leave Florida, despite having had a great time, I started counting down the hours until I could see Brody. I knew the separation had been good for both of us, but that didn't make me any less excited to be with him again.

Brody needed lots of exercise, and we have a beautiful, wooded trail just a few minutes from our home where I can take off his leash and let him run free. Sometimes just the two of us went, other times Marty and Max came along. Often Brody would pick up a stick, run with it, drop it, and then choose a new one. Occasionally he'd choose a stick that was three or four feet long, then come running on the trail from behind. I suppose this would qualify as a branch. I'd look back and shout, "Watch out!" and Marty and I would jump off the path before Brody ran by.

My brother once took this walk with us and didn't realize in time that getting hit with a branch was a possibility. Luckily, he wasn't hurt, just surprised. I didn't think this obsession with sticks was a good habit, but I wasn't sure how to stop a dog from playing with sticks in the woods.

One weekend, Brendan and Louise stayed at our house, so all six of us went for this walk. Brody was running along the trail when he suddenly stopped moving. It is not normal for Brody to stop moving in the woods when he has freedom. Everyone gathered around him to see what was wrong.

Louise said, "Blood is coming from his mouth."

Brendan held Brody from behind and opened his jaw.

Marty looked in his mouth and said, "I see it." Then he pulled a four-inch stick from Brody's throat. Once the stick was removed, Brody ran off as if nothing happened. This was a terrifying experience. What if I'd been alone?

The next time we entered the woods, I was watching and waiting for Brody to pick up a stick as he always did. My plan was to shout, "No!" and make him drop it. But for the entire loop through the woods, Brody never touched a single stick. I was amazed and pleasantly surprised. To this day, Brody has never picked up a stick again. This shows that he learned from his experience and that the memory has stayed with him.

*　　*　　*

It was getting closer to April 10th, which would have been Kelsey's thirtieth birthday, and I was growing more anxious. How could I honor her? And how would I even get through the day? I was sitting in Patty's kitchen when she asked, "Was there anything Kelsey really wanted to do that she never had the chance to?"

My immediate thought was the marsh trail. I had discovered this wonderful hike shortly after Kelsey got Brody; I'd been looking for a place where he could run off-leash, and a friend mentioned the Willie Wildlife Marsh Trail. It was about twenty minutes from Kelsey's house. At the beginning of the trail is a bridge that crosses a stream. After walking about fifteen minutes next to the marsh waters, you turn left and go over two huge bridges that cross the entire body of water. When I stop on the bridge to admire the view of cattails, lily pads, ducks, geese, a beaver lodge, and an occasional blue heron, Brody jumps up on his hind legs and puts his front paws on the rail. He stands beside me gazing out at the water, as if he too is enjoying the view. After the second bridge there's a loop that goes to the back side of the water where there are benches to sit and Brody's favorite place to swim.

At least a dozen times during Kelsey's last summer, I'd find her asleep on the couch. I'd nudge her awake and say, "I'm taking Brody to the trail. Why don't you come with us?" I knew Kelsey couldn't handle our usual route, but there were other choices. I tried to encourage her, saying, "We'll just walk straight in on a flat path, you'll get to see Brody swim and then we'll leave."

Kelsey always said, "I'm too tired. Maybe next time."

So I'd put Brody in my car and drive to the trail without her. As we walked, I'd have him sit on the bridges, and I'd send Kelsey pictures. When we got to the bench, I'd send her videos of him swimming.

Now, Patty and I decided to walk Brody and Baine, her plot hound, on this marsh trail for Kelsey's birthday. It felt good to have a plan, and I knew this is what I'd always do on April 10th. Then I thought about how Marty had tied my hairband to a tree at Devil's Tower and we'd said a prayer for Kelsey. I wanted to replicate this idea and tie some prayer cloths for Kelsey on the marsh trail.

First, I took pictures of many of her favorite things—dresses, skirts, sweatshirts, the plaid coat she wore sitting with Marley, her artwork, a blanket she kept on her bed, and the yearbook cover she designed. Then I had each pattern put on a 6-inch-long piece of stretchy fabric that would work perfectly as prayer clothes. I also had the patterns put on bandanas for Brody to wear. When he's wearing the orange bandana with a silhouette of black flowers, I see Kelsey in this floor length dress on a night we went out to dinner in Arizona.

For Christmas one year, Kelsey had asked for a very expensive hoodie. She said, "It's on sale for half price but my size is out of stock." Every few days, I'd gone on the website to check. Her size had never become available before Christmas, but when it became available in February, I ordered it. Kelsey was surprised when she opened a present for what would be her last birthday and there was the hoodie. Now, when Brody wears the cream-colored bandana with a paisley pattern of light blues, pinks, and greens, I hear Kelsey saying, "Thanks Mom! I can't believe you remembered." He has a whole collection of these for me to choose from. Each bandana is a memory and a literal connection to Kelsey.

Just days after Kelsey's funeral, a man named John had been helping us design Kelsey's headstone—another jarring expectation, when my mind was still trying to turn back time and not open that kitchen door. John had told us we needed to decide on the color and shape of the marble we wanted. Marty, Brendan, and I were forced to go outside to look at samples and make choices. We chose black marble, rough edges, and two vases attached to the base with simple crosses etched into them. Then John held up a small oval shape and asked, "Would you like a picture of your daughter placed above her name?"

We hadn't known it was an option to have an actual photo adhered to the stone. Marty and I looked at each other and both said, "Yes. The picture of Kelsey with Marley."

At our previous home on Brower Road, there was a group of boulders Marty strategically placed with the tractor to look decorative. When I took the picture, Kelsey was sitting on a boulder wearing her favorite plaid coat, with Marley sitting in front of her. The leaves in the background show their beautiful fall colors. I always loved her smile in this picture and how her blonde curls perfectly framed her face. As much as I could, I felt uplifted knowing this image could be on her gravestone.

Near the end of the appointment, Marty had asked, "When will this be finished?"

Before choosing this memorial place, I'd made several calls and learned it was too late for a headstone to be put in before winter. At first, this news had really bothered me, but then I felt resigned; what difference did it make?

I hadn't shared this information with Marty. So when John told him the cemeteries close for winter, with the weather determining when he's allowed back in—and that the marble comes from Vermont, and they don't even ship it until early April—Marty was visibly upset. He said, "Kelsey's birthday is April 10th. Is there any way the stone can be in place before her birthday?"

John could tell how important this request was to Marty. He said, "I'll drive my own truck to Vermont in March and pick up the marble for your daughter's stone. I can't promise, but I'll do my best to have it in place before April 10th." At the time, we were touched by this kindness from a person we'd just met. It made one of the worst days of all our lives the tiniest bit more bearable.

Now, many months later, John called just a few days before Kelsey's birthday. He said, "The headstone will be placed at the cemetery tomorrow." True to his word, John had driven to Vermont in March with his own truck instead of waiting for the marble to be shipped.

I thanked him repeatedly, though even thanks didn't seem like enough for such a kind act.

I knew I wanted to be alone the first time I saw the headstone. I waited for Marty to leave for work, then drove to the cemetery. There is nothing that can prepare a parent for seeing their child's name on a headstone.

I stared at the date: September 28th. The 26th had been a Monday, and, I knew now, my last day with Kelsey. It had been an ordinary day for us. When I'd gotten to the house, Kelsey had even told me she was feeling a little better. I felt hopeful that maybe this bad spell of worsening symptoms was improving. We put Brody in his crate and drove to her general practitioner's office to meet with a person from the spinal cord stimulator company. The system had been turned off for years, but I thought: *Why not give it another try?* We discussed this with the representative.

After the appointment, Kelsey said, "Could we walk around Target for a little while?"

"Not today," I told her. "My stomach has been bothering me." How I wish I could have that moment back.

When we got to the house, I took Brody for a walk. My stomach still hurt, but he needed exercise. Kelsey said, "Before you leave, would you make me scrambled eggs and toast?"

I'm glad I said, "Sure."

After I handed Kelsey the plate, she said, "Thanks for the eggs, and for taking Brody for a walk. I love you."

I said, "Love you, too. See you Wednesday."

It was about 5 PM when I left. Before leaving, I reminded Kelsey that the next day, Tuesday, I'd be working at the co-op in Albany where my jewelry was for sale. Less than two days later, I'd find Kelsey. I left the cemetery hoping the shock of already having seen her name on the stone had better prepared me for seeing it again with Marty.

The morning of April 10th was finally here. I'd been feeling so much anxiety in anticipation of this day that I felt somewhat relieved. I drove with Brody to the marsh trail as planned. Patty and Baine arrived just a few minutes after we pulled into the parking lot. It was a beautiful, sunny day for April. Once we were safely away from the road, we let the dogs off their leashes. They both took off running in that jubilant way dogs do when they have their freedom.

Brody knows it's time to swim when we get to the open stretch of land near the benches. The water was still mostly covered with ice, but there was a small area that had thawed. Even though the water must have been freezing, he jumped in for a brief swim. This is his favorite place along the trail, which is why I wanted to tie the prayer cloths here. I walked behind the bench, crossed the ditch, and chose a tree out of view from the trail. Then I tied three prayer clothes to its branches and said a prayer for Kelsey. Now, whenever I return to the trail, I can visit that tree knowing they were placed there on her birthday.

When I climbed back across the ditch, Patty was sitting on the bench. "I met someone at a pet store who has a therapy dog," I explained. "She gave me a card with a picture of her dog on the front and a story about him on the back. I want to do something like that to tell Kelsey and Brody's story."

Patty said, "Why don't you make a bookmark?"

I loved this idea. Then it would be a useful gift.

As soon as I got home, I looked up companies that made bookmarks you could design. Even though Brody and I hadn't passed the test yet, I designed a bookmark with three pictures and ordered a small batch to make sure they were well made. At the top of the bookmark is a picture of Brody taken when Kelsey and I first brought him home. He is sitting on his dog bed and weighs only 7 pounds. In the middle, there's a selfie Kelsey took of Brody pressed against her cheek while they were on the couch together. At the bottom is a picture of Brody on the dock from the day Kelsey came out on the boat with us.

On the back of the bookmark, it says: "Brody was just two months old when he met Kelsey on April 18, 2021. She wanted Brody to become a therapy dog when he got older. Kelsey was diagnosed with autonomic small fiber neuropathy, and passed away on September 28, 2022, when she was 29. Brody now brings happiness to the people he visits in her memory.

I wanted to say more, but there isn't a lot of room on the back of a bookmark.

When Brendan was finished with his workday, he came to our house so the three of us could go to the cemetery together. I looked at him and thought about how strange it was that he was almost a year older, and his sister was not. He still looked just like his father at this age, but, at six-foot-two, he towered over me. Whenever we hugged, it made me smile—still does, because he needs to completely bend over.

When I was young and dreamed of being a mom someday, I'd always been adamant that I'd never have an only child. Having three siblings myself, I'd always thought only children must be lonely. No matter how people get along with their siblings, they'll always be their closest family members. I'd already failed Kelsey in other ways, and now it felt like I'd failed Brendan, too, because I was leaving him in this world alone. At the same time, I was thankful that he had Louise, a great job, and a house he'd bought only an hour away. It would be easy for me to continue being an important part of his life.

One day, in my "After" life—the one in which Kelsey is missing—Brendan, Louise, Marty and I had gone on a hike. When we reached the summit, I looked at the gorgeous view and pulled out my Ziploc bag filled with prayer cloths. "Just reach in and pick one," I'd said to Brendan.

He did, not looking, and held up the chosen piece of fabric. I was stunned. "That's from the dress your sister wore to your college graduation!"

Brendan said, "I know. I remember." Then he tied the cloth to a tree branch, and we stood quietly for a few minutes, both lost in our thoughts.

At that moment, I was grateful that Kelsey had felt well enough to attend her brother's graduation and the celebration we'd had afterwards. I'm sure Brendan wouldn't normally remember what dress Kelsey wore. But there's a picture of the two of them from that day that I'd hung in the house years before Kelsey died, in which he's wearing a red and gray striped tie that perfectly matches the stripes in her dress. He had put on the suit in his dorm room, and she had gotten dressed at home. When they later stood beside each other, we all laughed because their matching outfits looked planned.

There were times, I knew, when Kelsey had been jealous of Brendan's health and his and my easygoing relationship. I knew she wished that she too was healthy, could go to college, have partners, and live a normal life like he did. But as Kelsey got older, she also was proud of Brendan and happy for his good fortune; they'd rarely argued anymore, and her jealousy seemed to fade.

Our drive to the cemetery was quiet. We walked slowly in a line towards the headstone. At first, the three of us just stood there, not sure what to do or say. There is no precedent for such a moment. Then we gave each other some private time and went to Kelsey's grandmother's grave, which is directly in line with hers and only two rows away.

So far, I'd managed to be stoic. I stood beside Marty once more before leaving, staring at Kelsey's name. Then I looked up and saw the pain in Marty's face mirroring my own. Somehow this made it hurt twice as much. When he put his arm around me, I fell apart and let myself cry.

Chapter Nineteen

Marty was walking by me in the kitchen with an armload of items to pack in the saddlebags on the motorcycle. We were going to ride to Lake George, have an early dinner, and then walk around the village. It would be the first time on the motorcycle since Kelsey died. He opened a small container and started searching for something. I saw sunscreen, hand wipes, headache meds, a phone charger, and then he found what he was looking for.

"Remember that time I took Kelsey to Lake George on the motorcycle?" Marty said. "We played games in the arcade. Then we traded our tickets in for prizes, and Kelsey gave me this plastic spider ring." Marty put the ring back in the container, where I know it will always stay.

Before, anytime we'd gone for a ride, I'd always sent Kelsey a message. It was the first thing I thought of when I got on the bike. The text would say, "I'm getting on the motorcycle. If you send a message, I won't be able to answer right away." While we were riding, I'd wonder if she was trying to contact me with a problem. The moment we stopped, I'd get off the bike and check my phone. This anxious feeling annoyed me. I'd wish I could go away for just one day and not have to worry about her.

This time, it was the opposite. When we parked the motorcycle at the restaurant in Lake George, there was no need to check my phone. I hadn't imagined it would be possible to miss that worried feeling so much.

Why did Kelsey die? I asked myself this question every day. Small fiber neuropathy is not supposed to shorten a person's life span. I knew the medical reason Kelsey died at that moment; she aspirated due to an intestinal blockage. The final autopsy report said her colon was enlarged and had displaced her diaphragm, which is a muscle that separates the thorax from the abdomen. As the diaphragm contracts, it increases the volume of the thorax, which inflates the lungs. Her enlarged colon and displaced diaphragm reduced her lung capacity. These findings explained why Kelsey had an increased heart rate and worsening fatigue that summer. I spent most of Kelsey's life doing research. Trying to solve the mystery of her illness was ingrained in my being. Now, even though she was gone, I didn't know how to stop.

With a list in hand of all the medical people I wanted to speak to, I first called the ENT doctor that Kelsey saw three times in the months before she died. The receptionist told me the doctor would call me back. I waited a day, and then another, but she didn't call. I called again, and then again, but still no reply. Sometimes they'd say, "The doctor is in surgery this morning. She'll call you this afternoon." I'd wait a week and call again. After several weeks went by, the office manager called and said, "The doctor's legal team has advised her not to speak to you." I never got to ask about the edema found in Kelsey's throat or the tertiary contractions in her esophagus. It stands to reason that a compromised airway would increase the likelihood of aspiration.

With no other recourse, I filed a complaint with the Department of Health. They first warned me that most of the time the paperwork is reviewed, and no investigation is warranted. I was surprised when I received a letter in the mail saying my case was assigned to an investigator. I called her on several occasions, even though I knew she couldn't tell me anything. She had been patient and kind, but each time I called, she reminded me, "When the investigation is completed, you'll receive a letter in the mail."

As more and more months went by, I'd become frustrated and call again. Finally, I asked her, "What is the longest time a case has taken to investigate?"

She replied, "Three to four years."

I'm still waiting. I've been told that one day I'll go to the mailbox and there will be a letter from the Department of Health. The letter will say "no misconduct was found" or it will say, "misconduct was found." That's it! That's all I'll ever know.

Sometimes I wonder which I'd prefer. If the letter says no misconduct was found, then I'll have no one to share the blame with. If it says misconduct was found, then I'll feel even more responsible because I chose to take Kelsey to a local doctor instead of going to Manhattan or a larger facility to make it easier for me. Either way, I lose.

I know a nurse who works for a group of gastroenterologists. When I explained to her the edema found in Kelsey's throat, she said, "At our office, Kelsey would have been sent to the hospital immediately because she had a compromised airway." I must constantly remind myself that no matter who I talk to and no matter what information I'm given, nothing will change the outcome.

We had never made it to the appointment with the Sjogren's specialist in October. Now, I called and asked if Dr. Avery would have diagnosed Kelsey with Sjogren's based on her test results. The nurse said, "Kelsey was never actually a patient here, so we can't talk about her." I kept calling, because I know that at medical facilities, if a different person answers the phone, eventually you'll get a different answer. With perseverance, I found a kind nurse who was willing to speak to the doctor on my behalf. She called back and said, "Dr. Avery said her test results would confirm a diagnosis of Sjogren's Syndrome."

When Kelsey was 23, a CT scan showed atrophy of her pancreas. When an organ atrophies, it means the healthy organ tissue has been replaced by fatty, damaged tissue. The radiologist said, "The only time I've seen a pancreas atrophied in a person this young is when that person had cystic fibrosis."

To diagnose cystic fibrosis (CF), doctors order a sweat chloride test. CF causes a defective channel in the sweat duct cells that doesn't allow chloride to be reabsorbed. As a result, sodium stays in the duct while chloride remains in the sweat. During this test, a chemical and a small amount of electrical stimulation is applied to the person's arm or leg. The stimulation encourages the sweat gland to produce sweat, which is collected and sent to a lab. Then the amount of chloride can be measured. People with CF have more chloride in their sweat than people without cystic fibrosis.

Kelsey went to a local hospital to have this test. A normal level of chloride is less than 30, borderline is between 30 and 59, and an elevated level is greater than 59. Her first result was 77. This is a positive result for cystic fibrosis. Whenever someone has a positive result, they repeat the test. Her second result 12 days later was 71. We were told that Kelsey had a mild form of cystic fibrosis. The doctor used the term mild because cystic fibrosis usually affects the lungs, and Kelsey had no history of lung issues.

Cystic fibrosis is a progressive, genetic disease. It affects the lungs, pancreas, and other organs. The cells that produce mucus, sweat, and digestive juices become dysfunctional. This causes these fluids to become thick and sticky. These fluids then plug up tubes and ducts.

Even if Kelsey's form was mild, this was a serious diagnosis, so we went for genetic testing. At the time, mid-40's was the average life expectancy of a person with CF. The genetic testing showed no mutation in Kelsey's CFTR gene, and we were told she didn't have cystic fibrosis. This was great news, but at the same time very confusing. Why did she have two positive sweat chloride tests and an atrophied pancreas? No one ever successfully answered these questions.

I always believed this was an important clue to figuring out what was wrong with Kelsey. It is abnormal for a young person's pancreas to atrophy, but her doctors didn't seem concerned. They said things like, "Well, her pancreas is working. No need to worry until it stops working." I disagreed with this approach, but everyone kept sending us away.

After Kelsey died, Boston Mass General agreed to have a pathologist test her pancreatic tissue post-autopsy. The report says (bear with me): "Pancreatic Parenchyma with atrophy, fatty replacement, and a focal mixed inflammatory infiltrate associated with degenerative acinar cells and intralobular ducts. CD4 and CD8 immunostaining reveal a CD8-dominant T cell infiltrate. There are patchy foci with PD-L1 expression in inflammatory cells and epithelial cells with rare, scattered PD-1+ lymphocytes. The overall findings raise a possibility of immune-related lobular injury."

What does this mean? The pathologist said Kelsey may have had an undiagnosed condition that caused her pancreas to atrophy, secondary to inflammatory cells attacking the pancreatic tissue. They also said that cystic fibrosis couldn't entirely be ruled out.

The Cystic Fibrosis Foundation was very helpful. When I asked medical questions about the disease, they gave me a phone appointment with a clinician. The clinician explained that the Cystic Fibrosis Foundation would consider two positive sweat chloride tests and an atrophied pancreas to be diagnostic for cystic fibrosis, regardless of negative genetic testing. Their guidelines state that the sweat chloride test is the "gold standard" for diagnosing cystic fibrosis, because it is 98 percent accurate and false positives are very rare. The missing 2 percent are mostly people who have a borderline result and might still have CF. Repeating a positive test is standard practice to validate the results. The clinician said, "Kelsey should have been seen by a gastroenterologist who specializes in cystic fibrosis."

Of course, I *had* taken Kelsey to a cystic fibrosis specialist after the positive sweat chloride tests, but he was a pulmonologist who discounted the tests because she didn't have lung symptoms. He also blamed the positive test results on Kelsey's small fiber neuropathy. When I shared this with the clinician from the Cystic Fibrosis Foundation, she said there is no correlation between SFN and positive sweat chloride tests.

The autopsy doctor said, "Kelsey's pancreas was severely damaged, and she wouldn't have been able to digest a meal properly." He wondered why she hadn't been prescribed digestive enzymes. It is hard to hear medical people tell me what should've been done for Kelsey after she died.

I was coming to see Kelsey's life as a giant flowchart with an endless number of boxes and arrows. Each arrow pointed to a medical decision I made, such as a new doctor, medication, or procedure. It stood to reason that somewhere out there, among a myriad of choices, was a path that would've led to a different outcome. An arrow on the flow chart with a decision that would have saved her life. I never found the right path and I ran out of time. It was, and still often is, the not knowing that consumes me. One day I hope I can let the mystery of

Kelsey's illness go. I don't think it's possible for me to solve it with her gone.

This wasn't intentional, but somehow, I found myself with social occasions three nights in a row. The first was a party with people I worked with at school. They all knew about Kelsey—many were even her former teachers—and some had made us meals when Kelsey was recovering from surgeries and shown warmth and concern at various times. I decided to go. Everyone there was kind and compassionate, but I was miserable the whole time, worrying I was making people sad, or that they might not know what to say to me.

The next night, Marty and I were presenting the Kelsey Marie Waffle Memorial Scholarship to a student who was an exceptional writer, as Kelsey had been. We stood on the same stage Kelsey had walked across the night she graduated from high school, and, as with her eulogy, Marty presented the award with amazing strength. My only role was to stand beside him at the podium, but even this made me uncomfortable and nauseated.

The third night was a friend's wedding. On our way, I texted Karen, whose daughter, Alyssa, had died of cancer. "I don't like going to places with large groups of people," I wrote, "because seeing me makes everyone sad."

Karen immediately texted back. "I completely understand what you're saying and feel it deeply and often. But I also believe it's good for others to see us able to continue, because we are proof that it's possible to survive even the deepest pain." Her words were insightful and gave me a new perspective. Karen works at a funeral home. I'd always thought that must be hard and wondered why she would do that to herself, but now I realized that she sees it as a gift. When working with a grieving family, she shows them that you can get through this. Later, Karen confirmed this; she said it gives her a purpose.

The morning after the wedding, I was relieved to wake up and not need to wear a dress or go mingle with strangers. Instead, Louise, Brody, and I went to meet Patty and Baine for a walk on the trails behind Patty's house. Seeing the dogs happy was just what I needed. Marcy, another friend who has two yellow labs, joined us. It looked like a dog party with all four dogs running through the fields.

After our walk, we headed over to Marcy's backyard, where she has a pool designed for dogs. It has a deck for the dogs to jump off from and a ramp for exiting the pool. Those agility classes must have helped Brody, because he hurried up the ramp to see what was there. At the top of the ramp, he saw a pool for the first time. Marcy threw toys in the water for Brody to retrieve.

I said, "Go get it Brody."

Brody wanted so badly to retrieve a toy that he started to whine, but he was too afraid to jump in. He loved to swim, but he'd never had to leap into the water before.

"Go get it!" I said again. "You can do it."

Brody couldn't stand the excitement any longer. He leaped into the water, retrieved a toy, and climbed out of the pool, using the ramp.

Once Brody figured out this fun game, he kept retrieving toys, but he wasn't using the exit ramp correctly. He was trying to climb on the ramp where the water was too shallow instead of using the ramp as a gradual incline.

I was wearing clothes, not a bathing suit, but I rolled up the legs of my yoga pants and said, "I'm going in."

I lowered myself into the cold water. Then I guided Brody onto the ramp where the water was deeper. This allowed him to exit the pool much more easily and safely.

"Good boy," I said, and I thought, What a relief to just do something simple like this! To have something just be easy. After that, Brody kept jumping in the water, retrieving a toy, and climbing out, excited to do it again and again.

Eventually I got out of the water and put Brody's leash on to give Baine a turn. Brody didn't like this at all; he whimpered watching Baine have fun instead of him. Finally, I took off his leash and let him retrieve a few more toys before we left, so he could leave feeling happy and accomplished—just as I did.

Chapter Twenty

I wanted to take one more class before Brody and I tried to pass the therapy dog test. It was called Intermediate Obedience. The class was held in a pet store after hours, when the store was closed.

Kristine was the trainer. "Pick an aisle," she said to five people and their dogs.

I picked the aisle we were closest to, then realized it was the treat aisle. Before Kristine continued, I moved, thinking how hard it would be for Brody to focus surrounded by hundreds of dog treats.

"This class is mostly about your dog learning the basic commands such as sit, down, stay, and come, but with only hand signals," Kristine explained. "No words allowed." Then she gave us directions. "Use a hand signal for sit and stay. Walk to the end of the aisle, wait, and then use a hand signal for come."

Brody already knew a hand signal for sit and stay. I walked to the end of the aisle and Brody stayed and waited patiently. Then I patted my chest with my hand which meant come. Brody hesitated, unsure of what I was asking. I patted my chest more excitedly. Then he ran to me, and I gave him a treat.

During the next few classes, Brody had to sit and stay with me out of sight—sometimes even leaving the room. Another lesson required Brody to sit and stay, but as I walked away, I placed a treat on the floor at the midway point. Once I reached the end of the aisle, I used a hand signal to tell him to come. Brody was supposed to run to me and ignore the treat on the floor. This was the only lesson he struggled with. He'd come to me as directed but stop on the way to eat the treat. Who wouldn't?

Kristine suggested that instead of placing the treat in the middle of the aisle, I place it off to the side. Then I'd show Brody that I had a treat in my open hand when I told him to come. He was much more successful with this plan and passed by the treat on the floor most of the time.

Another trainer helping with the class was named Makenzie. After class one night, I said to her, "I'd like Brody to become a therapy dog."

She said, "I've taken the test to be a handler for a friend's therapy dog. I can give you and Brody private lessons if you'd like."

This was perfect. "Yes," I told her. "That's just what we need."

Makenzie and I planned to meet at my house for the first session, and then to meet at public places that allow dogs. At all our training classes, Brody did a great job, but he still jumped on people when he greeted them. This was the main skill we needed help with.

Sometimes a dog needs a lot of repetition to learn a skill or understand what they're being asked to do. The instructors were impressed with how quickly Brody learned. On the last night of class, he easily passed the intermediate obedience test.

The next week, we met with Makenzie at my house. Brody remembered her from class; I knew this because he piddled on the floor a bit when she arrived. He also jumped on her. "Give Brody his hand signal for sit when he's a few feet away from me," Makenzie suggested. "Once he's calm, wave your hand towards me and tell him to say hi."

We practiced this two-step process several times. Brody immediately picked up on the routine and stopped jumping on her. He was two years old. We'd been struggling with him jumping on people all this time, and Makenzie came up with a solution within minutes. This gave me hope that we could pass the test with her help. We picked a date and time for our next session in a public place.

One morning Marty called from work and asked me to drop something off at the college. He said to find his truck when I arrived and put what he needed on the driver's seat. I thought this was the perfect opportunity to walk Brody around campus and practice greeting people, as Mackenzie had shown us. I put Brody's Therapy Dog in Training vest on him for the first time and chose a bandana for him to wear that looks like Kelsey's plaid winter coat in shades of purple. After finding Marty's truck, we started walking around the campus.

It was a nice day, and a lot of students were outside. Brody looked handsome and confident as we approached a few groups of students sitting at picnic tables. "This is Brody," I explained to them. "He's training to become a therapy dog and is practicing how to greet people. Can he say hi?"

They were more than willing to help. We walked around the tables giving each person a turn to pet Brody. Each time I had him sit first, then told him to say hi. He was clearly loving all this attention. Then we made two loops around the campus. Brody greeted students who were walking between buildings or to the parking lot. The whole time we were there, he didn't jump on anyone.

I was about to leave but decided to give Marty a call. I knew he was teaching a class and wasn't sure if I should interrupt. But Marty said, "I'd love for my class to meet Brody." He told me which building and room number they were in, and we headed that way.

Brody wasn't at all intimidated when we walked into the room full of students. After Marty introduced us, I said, "Brody just took a training class. Let me see if he'll follow directions with such a big audience."

Using only hand signals, I told Brody to sit, lie down, and stay. I dropped the leash and walked across the room, then patted my chest for him to come. Brody ran across the room to me. The students were clearly impressed. We said goodbye to Marty and his class. Greeting people politely is the most important skill for a therapy dog. This was such a successful day that I started to have confidence.

Brody and I got ready to meet Makenzie at a store. I put Brody's Therapy Dog in Training vest on him and a bandana with blue diamonds that looks like Kelsey's favorite skirt. First, we walked around the store letting Brody get used to his new surroundings and the unusual noises. The huge floor cleaning machine went by, making swishing sounds. Brody was startled when we walked by a lift that beeped loudly when it moved. For the first ten minutes, Brody kept looking around, distracted, but then he calmed down and was able to focus.

Now all we needed were people willing to say hi to Brody. It's funny how you can tell right away if someone is a "dog person" or not. If a customer or worker seemed interested in Brody, I'd say, "He's learning how to be a therapy dog. Would you be willing to let him say hi?" Most people said yes. Brody greeted more than a dozen people and didn't jump on anyone.

After a few more sessions, we both felt Brody was ready to take the test. He no longer needed to sit first when greeting someone. All I had to do was wave my hand towards the person and tell Brody, "Say hi." Then he walked forward and put his head near the person, so they'd pet him.

The night before the test, I had the same feeling I used to have before a college exam. I was nervous and had trouble sleeping. Dogs are very perceptive; I needed to relax, or Brody would sense my anxiety. I thought about how much Kelsey wanted this for him and reminded myself that I needed to be a strong leader. I opened the box of bandanas and chose the one that looked like the yearbook cover Kelsey designed. Then, when I looked at Brody during the test, I'd remember how proud we were of Kelsey, and how proud she was of herself when all her classmates were walking around the middle school with that yearbook. Before walking into the store, I took a few deep breaths and told Brody, "We can do this!"

Inside, Makenzie said, "Walk at a normal pace, a slow pace, and then walk really fast while making left and right turns."

The point of this was for Brody to stay by my side on a loose leash and follow my lead, no matter what I did, without resisting or pulling. He did this successfully.

Brody then greeted a child, a seated person, and customers walking around the store. He did a great job, just as we'd practiced.

"We're taking a dog therapy test," I said to a young man who was working. "Would you mind running by us while we're walking?" This was also listed on the test.

He agreed. Brody didn't care at all when he ran past us.

Makenzie said, "Would you mind doing it again? But this time run faster."

The worker was being a good sport, even though he looked a little embarrassed by this request. When he went running by us at full speed, Brody didn't lunge at him or react in any way.

A section on the test tells the evaluator to handle the dog's head, body, tail, paws, throat, and ears. Brody finds this activity enjoyable, as if he's getting a massage.

An important skill is how Brody reacts to other dogs. For this part, Makenzie had asked someone to bring their dog and meet us at the store. She told us, "Go ahead and walk by each other." Brody walked by the other dog several times without wavering from my side. He never barks at other dogs or reacts negatively.

The test had nine sections, with 38 yes or no questions. The handler and dog must have all check marks in the "yes" column to pass the test. Brody passed! I left feeling incredibly proud of him. I also felt grateful that we'd met Makenzie. She was an integral part of getting us here. Now I'd be able to submit our application to Alliance of Therapy Dogs for their approval.

Ever since Brody had come to live with us, I'd been hoping for this moment. When we got home, I thought I'd feel like celebrating. Instead, I felt an overwhelming sadness. Brody and I were a therapy dog team without Kelsey. I was his handler, not her. This was the last goal she'd had in life. Just like all her other dreams, this one never came true. The void I feel every day of missing her just felt bigger that day.

A couple of weeks later, an envelope arrived in the mail. Brody's application was approved. Inside the envelope was a red heart-shaped tag to be clipped on his collar whenever he enters a building for a visit. The tag said, "Therapy Dog."

I started making phone calls to facilities for us to visit. I also tried to answer a difficult question: Should I take Brody to the hospital where Kelsey, Marty, and I spent 49 days that left us all traumatized? At first, I thought, *No way.* Just driving by the hospital made me feel ill. Why should I put myself through that? It would be impossible to walk those halls and not relive all those awful memories.

But then I reconsidered. The purpose of being a therapy dog team is for Brody to bring happiness to patients. I know how much Kelsey would've enjoyed being visited by a therapy dog during her hospital stay. Finally, I decided to apply as a volunteer, thinking the experience might be good for me. Part of the application process required sending a picture of Brody for his identification tag. I put a bandana on him that showed a painting Kelsey made, then we went in the backyard for a photo shoot.

We were given an appointment with the director of the volunteer department. When Brody and I pulled into the hospital parking lot, all I could think about was Kelsey. Aside from our extended hospital stay, we'd been here many other times. She'd seen a gynecologist, a urologist, and a neurologist here. She'd had multiple procedures at this hospital, and we'd frequently used their lab for blood work. I remembered her last appointment, an EMG to see if her small fiber neuropathy was affecting her large nerve fibers.

As Brody and I walked down the main hallway, I got teary and worried I might start crying uncontrollably. My stomach hurt; it was hard to breathe. My head started pounding. I thought, *What am I doing here?* I wondered if Kelsey would think Brody and me doing this was a good idea or not. I wasn't sure. To get to the volunteer office, we had to walk around the cafeteria where Marty and I got Kelsey her favorite meal—pancakes and bacon. I shook my head. Why had I come back?

But the moment we entered the volunteer office, people gathered around us happily. "Is this Brody?" they asked, as if he were already a superstar. I was impressed that they not only were awaiting our arrival, but also knew his name. People immediately started petting him, and as usual, he loved the attention. My attitude started to change. Granted they were excited to meet Brody and barely noticed me, but I prefer not to be noticed.

The director started walking us around the hospital. She pushed the elevator button, and Brody stepped in like he'd been born on an elevator. I was grateful for all the practice he'd had while staying with Brendan and Louise at their apartment. The director took us to a bunch of different offices. She'd walk in and say, "This is Brody. He's here for his interview."

Every time she said this, I chuckled to myself. All morning Marty had looked at Brody and asked him, "Are you ready for your interview?" I had no idea our visit would be considered an interview. This was a good thing, because if I'd known, I would have been a lot more nervous. But as we walked around, this made sense to me. At each office, I'm sure the director was watching to see how Brody interacted with the employees before she'd allow us to visit patients. I was worried that Brody might jump on someone with all the excitement, but he didn't.

At one point, we walked into a room full of residents sitting on couches absorbed in their laptops. When they noticed Brody in the

Resident's Lounge, six or seven people gathered around him. Then they all started speaking to him in happy, high-pitched voices. Brody's tail started wagging like crazy and all I could think was—please don't pee on the floor. I was relieved when we left the lounge pee-free.

We walked back to the volunteer office to do some paperwork. It felt like the interview was over and Brody had passed. The director explained that our first visit would be with another dog handler and her therapy dog. That person would show me the steps I needed to know before we could visit with patients on our own. By the time Brody and I left, I'd begun thinking that coming here was not only okay but could even be therapeutic for me. Walking around the hospital and making patients happy would allow me to form new memories—and, as with my friend Karen, to have a purpose again.

Since Kelsey died, working on Brody becoming a therapy dog has given me that and much more. He's been my daily companion and helped me cope with many challenges I didn't want to face. It's bittersweet when I acknowledge that these were the very things I'd hoped Brody would do for Kelsey. Every day I look at him and feel grateful that he's in my life. It also makes me want to thank Kelsey. Brody was her last gift to me. I'm not sure I could have survived this without him.

Part III

Chapter Twenty-One

Brody had been opposed to getting in the car lately. I would open the door, and he would back away and refuse to jump in. This baffled me, because we always went to fun places. I read about dogs with car issues and tried many of the suggestions, but nothing improved the situation.

The day before our first official therapy dog visit, Marty and I were leaving the house, and Brody was coming with us. Even though I was tossing treats around, he refused to get in the car. I'm not supposed to force him, but I bent over to lift his front paws and place them on the backseat. While I was bending over, Brody jumped up, and our heads collided. Brody was fine; I was not! My right eye instantly swelled. Within hours, the skin around my eye was a deep shade of purple with tinges of blue.

"How do I show up for our first therapy dog visit with a black eye?" I asked Marty. "People are going to ask questions." I wasn't saying this in an angry way. It wasn't Brody's fault. The truth is, I found the situation funny—what a memorable way to begin our career as a therapy dog team.

The following day my eye looked even worse. It was more swollen, and now there were shades of green mixed in with the purples and blues. I've seen people in movies cover up their black eyes with makeup. I doubted this would work, but I had no choice. I dabbed on the tinted cover-up carefully, because it hurt to touch the bruised skin.

When I was finished, I couldn't believe how good it looked. I walked out to the kitchen to show Marty. "What do you think?" I asked.

"If I didn't know it was there," Marty said, "I wouldn't even notice."

This was great news. I put on Brody's heart-shaped dog tag and the bandana that looks like Kelsey's plaid coat. This one tends to be my favorite. During the wintertime, Kelsey wore this coat everywhere she went for many years. We have so many pictures of her wearing it: in New York City, at a cookout in the woods on Brower Road, holding her cousins when they were babies, sitting next to Marley. When Brody wears that bandana, I see Kelsey, and I'm filled with memories.

Even though Brody had passed his interview at the hospital, I was still waiting for them to coordinate a meeting with another handler. This person and their dog would walk around with Brody and me, since we hadn't yet met with patients.

Instead of the hospital, our first therapy dog visit was at a beautiful facility for mostly independent women who live with minimal assistance. I arrived there early to walk Brody before going inside.

Meagan, the activities director, brought us to a living room where ten women were seated in a large circle.

"My name is Debbie Waffle, and this is Brody," I said. "This is our very first therapy dog visit."

Meaghan and I had spoken ahead of time about whether I should tell the women about Kelsey. She said it was up to me, but she thought they would appreciate hearing it. I gave Meaghan a handful of bookmarks to pass out while I talked.

"I got Brody for my daughter, Kelsey," I explained. "She had a condition called small fiber neuropathy and passed away suddenly last September. Kelsey had wanted Brody to become a therapy dog someday." I felt confident I could tell the story without crying, but I struggled a bit near the end.

The women were kind and expressed how sorry they were for me, Brody, and our family. Everyone looked at the bookmark. Someone asked, "Is that Brody as a puppy? He's so tiny."

I said, "Yes, in that picture he weighed just 7 pounds."

"What kind of dog is he?" another woman asked.

"He's a golden retriever," I said. "And he's only two years old. So still a bit of a puppy."

All this time, Brody and I were standing at the front of the room. I began walking around the circle and letting each person pet Brody for a few minutes. Then we walked around the room a couple more times talking with the ladies.

"He's beautiful!" the women kept saying. "He's such a good boy."

Someone asked about the scarf Brody was wearing. I said, "I took pictures of Kelsey's favorite clothing and had the patterns put on bandanas for Brody to wear. This bandana is a picture of a winter coat she loved. I wanted to figure out a way to feel like Kelsey was a part of our visits."

As we said goodbye, Meaghan said, "Brody did a great job."

I drove home with Brody in the backseat, thrilled and relieved our first visit had gone well. And thankfully, no one had noticed my black eye—or if they had, they hadn't said anything.

The next morning, Marty said, "You guys are famous." He showed me that Meaghan had put pictures of Brody and me on their Facebook page. In each picture, Brody is politely sitting or standing next to someone being petted. By the end of the day, he had a following of people that liked his pictures and commented on our visit.

Next, Brody and I went to the hospital for our first visit with patients. We met Nicole and her border collie, Tate. She would show me the steps I needed to follow each time we came to the hospital. First, I'd log on to the computer as a volunteer; then I'd grab the clipboard with the list of patients who signed up for therapy dog visits. The list at first glance was overwhelming.

"I usually stay for about two hours and then call it a day," Nicole explained. "You check off who you visited, and the office updates the list."

When we left the volunteer office, Brody was totally at ease walking beside Tate, even though they'd never met before. Nicole looked at the list and picked a place for us to start. I couldn't believe it when we stepped off the elevator and entered the urology wing. The hospital has five patient buildings, a total of 21 floors, and 766 beds. Our first visit with a patient was in a wing that Kelsey, Marty, and I had spent a significant amount of time in.

But walking around the urology wing made me realize I'd made the right decision. I could clearly picture Kelsey lying in bed, trying her best to deal with the pain, but I also imagined how much she would have appreciated a visit with a therapy dog. And that gave me the encouragement I needed.

As we walked around, many of the staff noticed that Brody was a dog they'd never met before. "Who is this adorable dog?" they asked.

"This is Brody," I told them. "He's a two-year-old golden retriever."

"Only two years old?" People were always surprised by his age. "My dog at two was never this well behaved." We heard this over and over.

"I love how red his fur is," patients and workers kept saying. "You don't often see golden retrievers whose fur is this deep shade of red."

I gave the bookmark about Kelsey and Brody to some patients, visitors, and staff. When we returned to the volunteer office to sign out, Nicole told people that Brody had done an amazing job and was a wonderful therapy dog.

*　　*　　*

Brody and I returned to the hospital two weeks later for our first solo visit. I logged into the computer and headed out with the clipboard in hand. Staff members were excited to see us return. As we were coming down the hall, a nurse remembered us and announced, "Here comes Brody!" She visited with him and told me she had hung Kelsey's bookmark on their bulletin board.

An elderly man was sitting in a wheelchair when we entered his room. He said, "Brody reminds me of a dog I had as a child." Then he talked for a long time, telling me stories about this dog he loved. When we left, the man said, "Thank you. I haven't thought about that dog for a long time."

We entered a room that was totally silent, no television on and no visitors. A woman was lying in her bed looking sad. When she noticed Brody, she smiled, and her eyes brightened.

"Would you like a therapy dog visit?" I asked.

"Of course," the woman answered.

Brody walked alongside the bed and stood. The woman's hand was flat against the sheets with her palm up. She had limited mobility and did her best to lift her arm and pat him with the back of her hand.

I said, "Would you like Brody to sit on a chair so you could see him better."

The woman looked surprised. "He can do that?" she asked.

I opened a folding chair beside her bed and tapped the seat. Brody jumped onto the chair and sat. The woman laughed and smiled. Now she could see him face to face and pet him more easily.

When it came time to leave, the woman said, "Thank you for visiting me. You're lucky to have such a wonderful dog."

We were new to the hospital. I was surprised when a nurse got on the elevator and said, "Is this Brody?" When we stopped at her floor, she gave Brody a hug. "Hope to see you later," she said as she exited. I had no idea who this woman was or where she worked in the hospital.

After visiting with several patients, we went to another department, and I recognized the woman from the elevator. As we approached the main desk, five nurses surrounded Brody, all petting him and telling him how beautiful he was. Then they showed me their bulletin board. It was covered with pictures of their own pets.

Just as Nicole had suggested, we turned in the clipboard after visiting patients for a couple of hours. As Brody and I walked to the parking garage, I felt a huge sense of accomplishment. We'd made a difference in the lives of the patients we visited. I'll never walk into the hospital and not think about Kelsey, but I was already making new memories that made me feel good. I knew Kelsey would be proud of Brody, and pleased he was living the life she had imagined.

A week later, I went to the mailbox and found an envelope addressed to me from the hospital. My first thought was, *Oh no, a long-lost bill.* I walked back to the house thinking I'd be spending the next hour on the phone with the insurance company. Instead, I found a Fall Newsletter from Volunteer Services at the hospital. I glanced at the first page, then left it on the kitchen counter.

A few days later, the newsletter was still sitting there. I read the cover article—something about a nonprofit organization that makes patchwork quilts for children facing serious illness—then started towards the garbage can to throw it away. As I walked, I turned the page. And there was Brody! He was sitting in our backyard, wearing a bandana that shows a painting Kelsey made–the photo I had sent in for his identification tag. The title above him said, "New Therapy Dogs in 2023". Brody's name was printed under his picture. The article welcomed us to the program.

The next week, Brody and I entered the hospital just as a woman was coming down the hall with her therapy dog. It was a miniature poodle, and he ran up to Brody, excited, and then under his belly and in between his legs. Brody looked terrified. He picked up each foot as the poodle scurried beneath him, then leaned against the wall trying to escape. The scene reminded me of a person with a mouse running around their feet.

I was laughing. "All his doggy friends are bigger than him," I explained to the woman. "He's never met such a tiny dog before."

Soon Brody relaxed, though, and the poodle sat on the floor beside him. While we were talking, the woman interrupted her own story and said, "Is this Brody from the newsletter?!"

It felt like he was a movie star. "Yes, it is," I said proudly.

Soon we added a residential health facility to the list of places we were visiting. Brody arrived wearing a blue and white checkered bandana that looks like a quilt Kelsey kept on her bed. We waited on the first floor near the elevator.

The elevator doors opened. Erin, the activities director, stepped into the hall. "Is this Brody?" she asked. I love the fact that hardly anyone knows my name, but they all know Brody's.

We went up to the third floor to work our way down. The residents were either lying in bed, sitting in a wheelchair, or going up and down the halls using walkers. This was very different from the hospital, where most patients are in beds.

Erin walked into each room and said, "Brody, our new therapy dog, is here!" She announced Brody like he was a superhero. I imagined him wearing a cape.

We stopped at room after room visiting with residents. One woman was blind. Her face lit up with a smile when she reached out and touched Brody's face. She ran her hands along his ears, the top of his head, and his neck.

Another woman asked me what Brody did. At first, I didn't understand her question. Then she clarified, "Does Brody know any tricks?"

Using only hand signals, I had Brody sit, lie down, then stand. I told him to shake with each paw. I put a treat on the floor, and he didn't eat it until I said, "Okay." The woman smiled. "Very impressive," she said.

We visited with a man who seemed a bit grumpy. But he perked up a little when we entered his room, and when we left, Erin said, "That's the first time I've seen him smile."

One person had a food tray near him with fries. Brody's nose turned toward the tray. I said firmly, "No!" He left the fries alone and stood next to the man's bed, choosing to be petted over snatching some fries—or at least obliging.

In another room we entered, a person had been eating chocolate cake, and a small piece had fallen on the floor. Brody lunged for the cake. I told him, "Leave it," and he turned around to visit the person.

Brody had been a therapy dog for just a few months. When Erin walked us to the exit, she said, "You'd think Brody had been doing this his whole life."

Chapter Twenty-Two

Just two weeks before Kelsey died, Brody and I had walked the marsh trail. On our way back to the house, I'd stopped at a sporting goods store.

When I got to Kelsey's house, she was sitting on the couch. I said, "I bought Brody a doghouse."

"Really!" Kelsey was excited. "He tries to stay out of the sun, but by late afternoon there's hardly any shade left. I think he'll love it."

"It will take me a while to put it together," I explained.

"Please don't let Brody see the doghouse without me!" Kelsey begged. "Let me know when it's ready, and I'll bring him outside."

I carried the box to the backyard and spread the pieces out on the lawn, sweating in the direct sunlight just as Kelsey had described. Putting the doghouse together was like a giant Lego project. Two pieces of the floor slid together. Then the four sides snapped in place.

The most difficult part was getting on the roof, which had a bunch of tabs. Eventually I realized a mallet would be helpful. I used it to tap the roof into place, which made it more secure. Then I moved the doghouse to a flat spot behind the house.

Finally I yelled from the back porch steps, "I'm done! Bring Brody out."

Kelsey opened the door and Brody came running. When he noticed something new in his yard, he eyed the doghouse suspiciously. Then he walked around it in circles.

I said, "Let me grab some treats." From Brody's treat jar in the kitchen, I grabbed a handful of tiny dog biscuits and hurried back outside.

I tossed a few biscuits on the floor of the doghouse, thinking this would entice Brody to go in. Instead, he ran beside the doghouse and stuck his head behind it, as if he thought the treats would come flying out the back. Kelsey and I laughed. Poor Brody—he looked so disappointed when it seemed to him that the treats had disappeared.

Next, I took a handful of treats and reached my arm inside the doghouse. Brody took his first step in and ate the treats out of my hand. Then he saw the other treats scattered on the floor, got excited, and ran around in circles snatching them up.

When Brody came out of the doghouse, I immediately threw in more treats. This time he hurried back inside without hesitating. He realized this fun game involved eating. As Brody continued going in and out of the doghouse, Kelsey took a video of him. This is the last video she ever took. You can't see her in the video, but you can hear her voice. She says, "There you go. Good boy, good boy!"

The doghouse came with a nameplate above the door and letter stickers. "Would you put his name on it?" Kelsey asked.

I nodded, then went into the house and found the stickers among the packaging. Back outside, I placed BRODY in the center of the nameplate.

While he stood next to the doghouse, Kelsey said, "Brody, sit." Then she took his picture. This is my last happy memory of Kelsey and Brody at the house.

When I first packed up her belongings after Kelsey's death, Marty wanted the house to look like Kelsey still lived there. To honor his request, I only removed the items inside cabinets, drawers, and closets. In a drawer, I found a birthday card she'd bought for me. Printed on the card, it said:

MOM,

I can't imagine

what life would be like

if I didn't have a mother

like you.

You've shown me the meaning

of unselfishness and the value of love.

It has always been a comfort

to know you're there

and that you'll always be there,

no matter what happens.

I've always been proud and grateful

that my mom is such

a remarkable woman.

I stood still, reading this. It was such a precious gift; especially given the guilt I'd been feeling, it was as if she'd left behind a special message for me to find.

In the mudroom, I left Kelsey's pink slippers beside the kitchen door. Some of her favorite clothes were neatly folded on a shelf. Family photos hung on the walls. Brody's treat jar sat on the kitchen counter; his doghouse was in the garage. Not until we were ready to sell the house did I remove the rest of her belongings and begin cleaning so it could be shown to prospective buyers.

Cleaning the whole house took several days. Each time, I had to reach into my purse, take out the keys, and open the kitchen door. Then I'd look over at the living room floor and relive that moment. There was nothing I could do to stop the memory from replaying. If I spent too much time in the house, I'd start to feel panicked, and I'd practically run to my car. Since September 28th, I've had only one comforting thought: *Kelsey is not in pain today.* This is what I kept repeating to myself as I cleaned.

I moved a chair from the kitchen table over to clean the window. When I saw the lower right corner, I gasped. It was covered with Brody's nose prints. I hesitated while holding the window cleaning spray, because I wanted so badly to leave them there. To me, they weren't just nose prints; they were part of a story that had ended.

Whenever I'd left this house, I'd told Brody I was going bye-bye. We'd meet in the kitchen where I'd give him a biscuit from his treat jar. Then I'd start to leave, but I always turned around and gave him one more treat and a hug. Once the door to the mudroom closed, Brody would hurry over to the kitchen window. I'd walk up to the window from the outside making sure Brody could see me, and wave. Then I'd keep looking back and waving at him until I got to my car. Brody would still be watching me as I pulled out of the driveway. This became our goodbye ritual.

I didn't want to do it. But I sprayed the window and removed those nose prints. It felt like another necessary part of saying goodbye.

The kitchen was the last room that needed to be cleaned. Now the house felt sterile, and all signs of Kelsey were gone. This was an awful feeling, but I also know it might make the place easier for us to sell.

The Realtor was having a photographer take pictures of the house to put online. He was meeting me there one day late in the afternoon. That morning, Brody and I met Patty and Baine at the marsh trail. When we got to the back side of the loop, the dogs ran into the water.

I'd only brought one floating toy. Patty held Baine while I threw the toy for Brody to retrieve. It is impossible to watch Brody swim without smiling and laughing. He flails his front legs up so high that they go above his head. This is not a productive way to swim. Instead of gliding through the water, it slows him down and he barely moves forward. Then it was Baine's turn. He swims low with his head staying just slightly above the water. Patty says he looks like a crocodile. Where the dogs swim is near Kelsey's tree. I climbed over the ditch to find the prayer cloths that were tied on her birthday.

While we were walking back to the parking lot, the photographer sent me a message asking if I could meet him much earlier than we discussed. I accepted his offer because it was supposed to rain later, which I thought wouldn't make for the best photos.

Patty said, "You go meet the photographer and I'll bring Brody home with me."

Brody hadn't been to Kelsey's house since that day. On a few occasions, I'd need something from there and Brody would be in my car. I'd park way up the road so he couldn't see the house, then leave him in the car for a few minutes. I'd asked Makenzie, the dog trainer, and she agreed—he should never go back. I think if Brody came into the house with me, he'd be confused and look for Kelsey.

When I arrived, the photographer was already there taking exterior pictures. Then we walked inside, and he asked me to open all the blinds to let the natural light in. He went from room to room taking lots of pictures. It didn't take long for him to get what he needed.

After he left, I had to walk around each of the ten rooms and close the blinds. This caused a wave of grief to wash over me. Taking pictures of the house felt like an invasion of Kelsey's privacy. The idea of strangers roaming around made me ill. When the house sold, I knew I'd have to say goodbye to Kelsey all over again.

I picked up Brody from Patty's, and we stopped at the cemetery. The picture of Kelsey and Marley had just been attached to the stone. It looked beautiful, but now I had to see her name and her gorgeous face and be reminded she was gone. Always the lows with the highs. I watered the flowers and went home.

We were grateful that the house sold in just a few days. Since Kelsey had lived there for only two years, it still looked new from all the renovations. Marty and I went there before the closing and wandered around crying in every room. It was torture to walk out that door for the last time. Because of its location, driving by the house is unavoidable. Now there is a white car in the driveway and a German shepherd in Brody's backyard.

The house was supposed to be Kelsey's future. As painful as it was to be there, it was still the place I'd felt closest to her. Now, visiting the house was no longer an option. This made me think about Manhattan, where Kelsey and I had traveled to for ten years. I felt the need to return there and retrace the steps we took together.

The trailer where I'd always bought our two roundtrip tickets was gone. Like most things today, you buy them online. My single roundtrip ticket was sent to my phone for the driver to scan. I wondered what became of the woman who'd sold the tickets from the trailer. For the entire ten years, it was always her.

It felt significant for me to make this trip alone. I'd never been to Manhattan by myself, but I found I had no fear. One morning, I left my house at 5 AM and drove to the Park and Ride in Ridgewood, New Jersey. I pulled into the parking lot before 8 AM and couldn't believe it was already filled. Usually if you got there before 8:00, parking wasn't a problem. Not only were there no parking spaces, but the lot was in total chaos. Some people had parked on the grass; others had decided to go over the curb and park among the trees that surrounded the lot. This behavior never would have been tolerated when the lady worked in the trailer. I decided to copy the people who had parked their cars along the exit ramp. This seemed risky, but so many people had already started the line that I felt there was safety in numbers. Another woman parked her car in front of mine just as a bus pulled in. We both took off running.

As we were running, the woman said, "I'm pretty sure we weren't supposed to park there."

I said, "I know, but what else could we do? I hope we don't get a ticket. Do you think he'll wait for us?" I was wearing sneakers. This woman was dressed in a skirt and high heels.

"He sees us," she said. "Hopefully he'll wait."

No parking spaces and not knowing if the bus would leave without me are negative things, yet I found myself smiling. These were things Kelsey and I had often experienced together. I let the woman in heels get on the bus first; the driver closed the door after he scanned my ticket.

People ride the bus to Manhattan in silence. On weekdays, they are a group of strangers on their way to work. No one says a word, which always made me a bit uncomfortable. If Kelsey and I got to sit together, we followed the rules and didn't speak to each other.

Now, there was a young girl sitting next to me. I whispered, "What gate number brings you back to the park and ride?"

She replied with a whisper, "Gate 408."

I was surprised that it was the same gate number it had always been. Because of Covid, Kelsey and I hadn't traveled to Manhattan during her last three years. All of her appointments had been virtual.

When I got off the bus, I was again surprised to find everything the same. I am probably the first person to stand in the main hall of Port Authority and openly cry in front of the smoothie place. Kelsey said they made the best smoothie she ever had. She'd get one on our way out of Port Authority and another on our way back. I continued crying as I walked to the exit, not caring what people might be thinking. That is mainly why I had wanted to go alone. I didn't want to feel the need to censor myself.

Kelsey and I had spent days in the city when it was pouring rain, freezing cold, or so hot the sweat poured out of us, especially in taxis without working air conditioning. Today, I walked onto the sidewalk and felt fortunate to have such a beautiful day. There was a clear blue sky, and the sun was shining.

I had always made her appointments in the afternoon, to ensure that we would be in the city early in case something went wrong. If we arrived with a couple hours to spare, we'd walk down Eighth Avenue. Now, I walked to Bryant Park, went into the shops, and waited. A few weeks ago, I'd arranged a meeting with Dr. Chambers, the pain management doctor. At noon, I took a taxi to his office, directly across from Central Park. I strolled around the park. It was busy with people walking their dogs and riding in horse-drawn carriages.

When it was our scheduled meeting time, I entered the office. I didn't sign the patient clipboard now, because I wasn't a patient, or with one. At the desk, I told the woman my name and wondered if anyone would know why I was here. The young man sitting next to her looked up from his computer when he heard me. I immediately recognized him. It felt good to see a familiar face.

He came out from behind the desk and hugged me. "I remember you and Kelsey," he said. "I'm sorry for your loss."

I hugged him back. "Thank you. It means a lot to me that you remember her."

He showed me to a room and said, "I'll tell the doctor you're here."

In the exam room were those same two little plastic chairs, sitting side by side. I sat in one chair and looked over at the empty seat where Kelsey would normally be. I couldn't stop staring at that empty chair. I had hoped not to cry, but that was a ridiculous expectation. It was such a relief when the door opened just a few minutes later. "I got your message," Dr. Chambers said, as he sat down across from me. "I can't imagine how difficult this must be for you."

An assistant who I also recognized came in with him. "I heard about Kelsey," she said. "I hope you don't mind, but I wanted to be here."

"Of course I don't mind," I told her. "I remember you."

She handed me a box of tissues. "Kelsey saw an unbelievable number of doctors," I said, and then I listed over half a dozen major medical facilities. "But only three took the time to know who she was and sincerely cared about her future. You were one of those doctors, and I wanted to thank you in person."

Dr. Chambers looked genuinely touched by my sincere compliment. He gave me a hug and said, "I really tried to help Kelsey."

"I know you did," I said.

"Do you want to tell me what happened?" he asked.

I shared Kelsey's cause of death and updated him on all the medical problems she'd had since we last saw him. I thought maybe I was taking up too much of his time; doctors are always in a hurry. But he just kept talking and asking me questions.

"How are you doing?" he asked. "You need to be taking care of yourself."

I said, "I have Kelsey's golden retriever. She wanted him to become a therapy dog. He passed the test, and now we're visiting hospitals and nursing homes."

"That's wonderful," said the assistant. "What's his name?"

"His name is Brody," I told them.

I thanked Dr. Chambers again for being a kind, caring doctor. They both hugged me, and we said goodbye. As I opened the door to the outside, it was hard to cross the threshold. I knew I'd never be back. Once more, it felt like I was leaving Kelsey behind.

A taxi drove me to Port Authority, and I stood in line at gate 408. In the afternoon, the buses come farther apart than during the morning and evening rush hours, but I waited only fifteen minutes before one pulled in. After the ride, I crossed the highway overpass in Ridgewood and spotted my car. No ticket. As I pulled out of the parking lot, I said aloud, "Goodbye Kelsey. I love you." Then I started the long drive home to where Marty, Max, and Brody were waiting for me.

Chapter Twenty-Three

I was watching a fictional TV program. One of the main characters had recently buried his son. Afterward, he'd become brazen, unpredictable, and reckless. When asked about his change in behavior, he explained: When you have buried a child, nothing else matters. This new reality brings with it a sense of freedom.

While no one would ever say I was unpredictable or reckless, I thought, *Whoever wrote those lines really gets it.*

After Kelsey died, I'd read even more memoirs—every book I could find about grief. I'd been surprised to discover that many of these were written by a parent whose child died. These stories helped the most, because not only did these people understand what I was going through, they also proved what I didn't think was possible—that there was a way to survive and even find meaning again.

In *The Grief Club*, by Melody Beattie, she explains how her twelve-year-old son died in a skiing accident. She writes: "You don't need to ask how long it has been because when you lose your child, it happened yesterday even if it's been ten years."

This was already apparent to me. As my first summer without Kelsey was coming to an end, it was inconceivable to me that she'd been gone for almost a year. In most ways, it felt, and still feels, like we were just at the gastroenterologist. I was just looking for a mallet to put the roof on Brody's doghouse. I can still see Marty taking a picture of Kelsey standing in front of the refrigerator wearing that green T-shirt.

Melody goes on to say, "Year two—worse. You want to be here even less." This statement scared me. How could year two be worse? I realized that everyone is different, and this wasn't an instructional manual, but still! Melody's son died in 1991, and her book was published in 2006. She is describing her personal experience with grief and the patterns she found after listening to other people tell their grief stories.

"Years three, four, and five," she writes "you still don't want to be here, but you keep waking up alive." My grief story was so young. It made me tired just thinking about the future Melody describes, but I also appreciated her honesty.

"Five through ten—gradually getting better each day. You've learned you can live with a hole in your heart." This wasn't a surprise. I already knew the hole in my heart would always be there.

*   *   *

Meanwhile, though, my work with Brody was keeping me going. One afternoon, Brody and I walked into a patient's hospital room. The female patient was lying in bed, and another woman was visiting her. Both had an open book in their laps. I introduced Brody as I always do. After having a brief conversation with these women, I decided it was the perfect opportunity to hand them Kelsey's bookmark.

Most of the time, people only focus on the front and admire the pictures. I never mention the story on the back, mainly because I don't want to make our visits about me; I want the priority to be the patient. But both women immediately turned it over and began reading. Then the woman visitor said, "My son passed away in a car accident 20 years ago. You should read a book called *Roses in December*."

She told me more about her son and asked questions about Kelsey. People who haven't yet experienced the death of someone they were close to often don't understand that many grievers want to talk about the person who died. They avoid bringing up their name and say things like, "I didn't mean to make you sad." You don't *make* grieving people sad. They already are.

That night, I downloaded *Roses in December: Comfort for the Grieving Heart*, by Marilyn Willet Heavilin, and started reading. It felt like Marilyn was speaking directly to me. Even though I read a digital copy in just a few days, I bought a hard copy because I wanted to look at the book's cover and remember its messages.

There were so many life lessons in her book that were inspiring, but I had a favorite part. A newly bereaved parent told Marilyn that it felt wrong to benefit in any way from their daughter's death. Marilyn explained that you could either be unaffected by the death, become a societal dropout, or become a better person because your child had lived and died. For me, there was only one choice. I want to be a better person because Kelsey had lived and died.

So, I ask myself: What has Kelsey's death taught me? Living with regret is hard. I can't think of an emotion that would be harder to live with. I will always regret how I treated Kelsey after she moved into the house: mostly my impatience. Now she isn't here for me to make it better. This has given me an awareness to make sure this doesn't happen again. When I go to sleep each night, I want to be sure that I won't feel regret if someone I love is gone the next day. We never know when we might be seeing or speaking to someone for the last time. Of course, I knew this before, but now I think about it on a regular basis.

I've learned not to let the little stuff bother me as much. Sometimes I find myself getting upset about something, and then I think, *Your daughter died. This is not a big deal.* With this mindset, things that seemed worthy of becoming unhinged or anxious about before now just don't matter. Everything difficult in life pales in comparison to burying a child.

At Thanksgiving, I typically feed about fifteen people. Before, I was always running around trying to make sure everything was perfect and ready at the exact same time. People would say to me, "What can I do to help?" My typical response was, "That's okay, by the time I tell you what to do, I could just do it myself."

After Kelsey died, my mom was at my house for Thanksgiving. She was there for about thirty minutes when she turned to me and said, "Why aren't you freaking out?"

I was leaning on the kitchen counter, feeling relaxed and talking to people. I replied, "Because it doesn't matter."

This doesn't mean I didn't care about making everyone a wonderful Thanksgiving meal. I just didn't feel the need to put so much pressure on myself, perhaps also at the expense of stressing out others. Instead, I focused on the moment and enjoyed the company of the people around me.

It had driven Kelsey crazy that I'd had always needed to be at least fifteen minutes early to everywhere we went. To me, being on time was late. If we weren't going to be early, I'd get myself all worked up and start to panic. She'd say, "Calm down, it isn't a big deal!"

Now, when I need to be somewhere, I'm either there at the required time or sometimes a few minutes late. I do this intentionally. It is a conscious decision that makes me think of Kelsey and smile. As I'm hurrying out the door, I imagine her saying, with a grin, "Really Mom? You couldn't do that with me, too?" Even though this doesn't necessarily make me a better person, it's still a valuable lesson that Kelsey taught me. She was seeing the big picture. I know Kelsey would be proud of me for this change in my behavior. She would appreciate that I'm not overreacting to such a trivial matter.

I've tried to make a difference by sending care packages to grieving friends, family, and even strangers as a kind act. Part of the package includes an enlarged picture I made of a sympathy card that just happened to come from Patty and Brian. The front of the card shows a silhouette of a huge tree with the sun setting in the background. The branches of the tree make the sun's orange glow appear to be sitting on the ground. In the upper right corner, it says: "You never know how strong you are until being strong is the only choice you have."

After sending a copy of this picture to many people, I became curious about the quote and looked it up. I was surprised to learn it came from Bob Marley—that's who Kelsey named our dog Marley after! Without knowing it, I had included a part of her story in the care packages.

I'm thankful that what would end up being Kelsey's last Christmas, we had a family gathering at her home a couple of weeks before the big day. She was proud to have Brendan and Louise over as guests. We ate a meal at her dining room table and decorated her tree. Then I gave Kelsey and Brendan a special present. They each opened a box filled with ornaments I'd made from favorite family photos. Each photo was mounted and framed with an assortment of Christmas ribbons.

Kelsey loved this gift! After opening it, she thoughtfully placed each ornament on her tree, making sure to put pictures of Marley or Brody front and center. I imagined Kelsey decorating her tree with those ornaments for many years, but instead she only got to use them that one time. Now I ask people to send me their favorite photos and include these ornaments in my care packages. When I make them for others, I feel closer to Kelsey.

On September 28th, the day Kelsey died, I was walking Max before driving to her house when my phone rang. The number wasn't in my contacts. For a moment, I stared at the screen and almost didn't take the call, but then as usual my curiosity won.

"Deb, this is Tricia," said the woman. "We met at a craft fair. Our booths were next to each other."

I did remember Tricia. Her booth was about homeopathic treatments, and she was there trying to get more clients. I had told Tricia about Kelsey's health problems, and we'd exchanged phone numbers.

Tricia said, "I woke up this morning and I couldn't stop thinking about you, for some reason. No matter what I did, you were stuck in my mind. Finally, I decided to just give you a call. Would you like to make an appointment for your daughter?"

I thought the last thing Kelsey and I needed was another appointment. "Thanks for calling," I said. "Kelsey is not doing well right now and it's hard for me to get her out of the house. If I make an appointment, we'd most likely end up canceling it."

She said, "Then maybe I can help you?"

I tried as politely as possible to say no, and we said goodbye. The whole time we were having this conversation, Kelsey had already died, but I didn't know it yet. Over the next few days, I kept remembering what Tricia had said, how she couldn't stop thinking about me on that morning, and her final words: *Maybe I can help you?* It felt like Kelsey had sent her to me.

A few weeks after Kelsey died, I called Tricia back, and we became friends. This friendship includes monthly visits for aromatherapy. When Tricia's father died, and then five months later her mother died, I visited her. She was struggling for obvious reasons. As soon as I got home, I started putting together a care package for her and put it in the mail when it was ready.

The following day my phone rang. It was Tricia. "I've been trying to call you for quite some time, but I had to wait until I stopped crying. I received your package. Thank you."

Tricia's mom had written a poem. In the package, I included my usual items, but I'd also had the poem her mom wrote put on a wall hanging. "I already hung the poem near my bed," Tricia said. "Now every morning I'll get to read my mom's beautiful message."

I said, "When someone is grieving, I want to remind them that they're not alone."

As time goes on, I know I will continue learning more from Kelsey.

My conversation with the woman at the hospital happened because I gave her Kelsey's bookmark. The book recommendation she made had a positive influence on my life. My hope is that when I've shared Kelsey's story, recommended a book, or sent a care package to a grieving person, that I too have made a difference during a chance encounter. Many times, someone has read the bookmark, and this has started a discussion about grief. When patients and staff share their own grief stories, I'm helping them. This is an added benefit to our visits that I didn't anticipate.

There is a website called codestiny.org. It was created by Joe Kasper after his nineteen-year-old son Ryan passed away in 2011 from an epileptic condition. Co-destiny is when a grieving person responds to the death of a loved one by taking on a new role in life. This way of thinking allows the grieving person to incorporate the lessons they learned so their life can move forward in a positive way that honors the person they have lost. With this mindset, the relationship with a loved one doesn't end with their death.

I feel fortunate to have found my co-destiny so soon. Each time we leave the house for therapy dog visits, I choose a scarf for Brody to wear that represents a part of Kelsey's life. Brody knows how to get from the parking garage to the volunteer office at the hospital on his own. This path includes seven hallways with a combination of three right turns and three left. One of the right turns is in a narrow hallway that I frequently almost walk by, but Brody always reminds me not to miss this turn.

During our two-hour visit time, we get on and off elevators constantly. One day, not long ago, we walked down a particular hallway where a group of nurses were gathered at the main desk. They were excited to see Brody, and they gathered around to pet him. I passed out a few bookmarks as we stood there chatting, then went to a patient's room on my clipboard.

About ten minutes later, a male nurse came into the room. He said, "After reading the bookmark, I had to come find you and give you a hug."

I was touched that Kelsey's story had such an impact. We hugged, and then he started to cry. I felt bad. "I'm sorry I made you sad," I told him.

He was kind and said, "I just love that Brody is here in her memory. I'm sorry this happened to you."

I again apologized for making him cry and thanked him for caring. Afterwards, I realized that I shouldn't have felt bad about this conversation, and I shouldn't have apologized. This implies that crying is something to be ashamed of. How brave of this man to cry because he felt such strong emotions!

When Brody and I are finished visiting with patients, we go back to the first floor. Brody immediately recognizes this is the floor with the parking garage, but he knows we first need to go to the volunteer office, where he gets a homemade dog treat from a cookie jar. I know this because Brody leads the way. Brody started out helping Kelsey; now, he helps lead me through my life.

On the same day we met the male nurse, I signed out on the computer and decided to go to the gift shop. This required making a left turn, when the parking garage was to the right. The leash suddenly became taut. I turned around to see what the problem was. Brody stood there with his front legs pressed against the floor. When I started to turn the "wrong way," he put on the brakes and refused to move.

This made me laugh out loud. These halls are busy places, and Brody was blocking traffic. I said, "It's okay, Brody, this way." He kept the brakes on a moment longer, wanting to make sure I knew the parking garage was the other way, but then he released his pose and walked beside me.

Brody has also become familiar with the routine at the residential facility we visit. It has three floors and a total of nine hallways. Unlike at the hospital, where we zigzag all over the place, here we go from one room to the next. Sometimes a person isn't in their room, is sleeping, or isn't a "dog person"; then Erin, who takes us around, will keep walking. This confuses Brody. He'll stop by the door we are skipping. You can tell he's thinking—*Why aren't we going in there? Maybe even, if you let me, I could cheer that person up!*

During a previous visit, Brody had passed up fries and crumbs of chocolate cake when I'd told him, "Leave it!" But one afternoon we walked into a patient's room, and he stuck his head under the bed before I had a chance to react. There he found and quickly ate a few pieces of crunchy cereal.

For the rest of that day, he stuck his head under every bed before visiting with the patient. Once Erin and I realized what he was doing, we both laughed. I told her about the stick in the woods and his incredible memory. I said, "I hope he doesn't spend the rest of his career looking under beds for cereal."

When we entered this facility again, Brody put his nose to the floor and started darting to his left and right searching for food. I thought, *Oh no, he remembers!* Luckily, after a few minutes of not finding anything edible, he gave up and focused on his job—getting petted by his adoring fans. Whenever we come home after visiting patients, Marty asks Brody, "Where's your paycheck?" This is one of those jokes that doesn't get old no matter how many times I hear it.

After Kelsey died, I wanted a way to feel connected to her as my life continued. When something special happened or I went to a memorable place or event with family and friends, I saved or bought something. I've collected dozens of items, which I keep in a box. Most of them are happy; some are sad.

Occasionally I sit on the floor, take out all the items, and think, *Kelsey, look at everything that's happened since you left.* I choose one item at a time, hold it in my hand, and remember where it came from, who I was with, and the memories associated with it. There's the newsletter from the hospital that welcomed Brody to the therapy dog program. On our last night in Ireland, eight women sat around a dinner table and shared their thoughts about this incredible adventure. I said, "I never thought I'd be brave enough to ride across Ireland on a horse!" It is this memory and so many more I think about when I hold the gold-colored Celtic bookmark I brought home. There are handwritten thank you letters from people I sent care packages to. They remind me that no one escapes grief and I'm not alone. When I hold the butterfly ornament from Bryant Park, it reminds me of the day I traveled to Manhattan and thanked Dr. Chambers. There's a prayer card for my Uncle Jimmy, who lived in Florida and died just ten months after

Kelsey. I'm grateful that Jimmy got to spend some time with Kelsey during her last summer. There are keepsakes from California, Hawaii, and Utah. When I've read a memoir written by a parent whose child has died, I've added their child's name to the collection. I know how important it is for parents living with this unimaginable grief to have their son or daughter remembered.

The woman who recommended the book *Roses in December* also said to me, "There's this grief metaphor about a ball and a jar. Look it up."

The metaphor says that grief is like a ball in a jar. The ball, which is your grief, never goes away and never gets smaller. It stays the same. But you, the jar, get bigger as time goes on and you're learning to live with the loss. The jar continues to grow as more time passes.

This visual representation of grief gives me hope. When Kelsey first died, my grief barely fit inside this tiny jar because I hadn't experienced anything new since that horrible day when I opened the kitchen door. I could barely move, barely think, barely breathe.

But since then, time has passed. My grief still feels like a heavy weight that I carry around with me, always there, never really changing. But now, when I sit among these items and all the memories they represent, I see that my life has continued without Kelsey. These objects show me that I'm still growing, still trying to be a better person because my daughter lived and died.

In the coming months, I'll make a return trip to the Jersey shore, something I've been avoiding. How could I be there without her? I don't expect it to be easy, but I know I'm ready. My late Uncle Jimmy has a son who is getting married. I'll travel to Florida for his wedding. I know how important it is to be surrounded by family when someone you love is missing. Brody will reach a milestone and earn a pin for having made 50 visits to medical facilities. He'll wear this pin on his scarves as we continue visiting with patients.

In the beginning, I wouldn't have thought it was possible, but now I know: My jar will keep getting bigger.

Photo Gallery

Kelsey, three months

With her father, Marty, after nursery school graduation

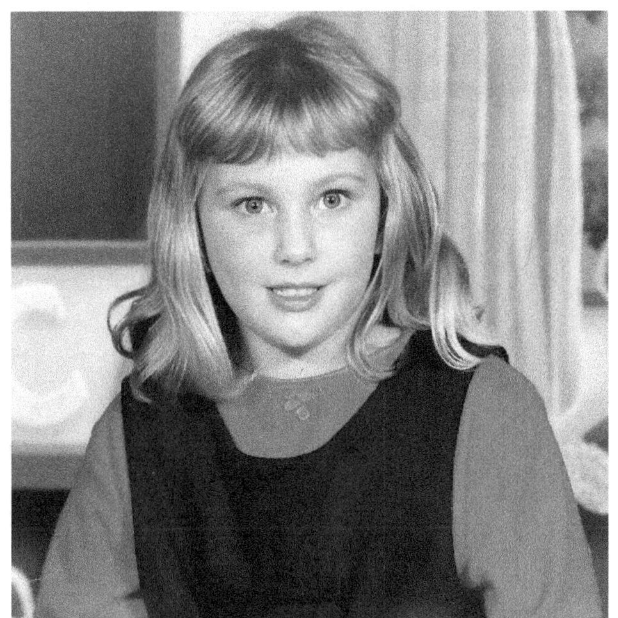

Kindergarten picture day

Kelsey and Brendan with Cocoa and Hershey

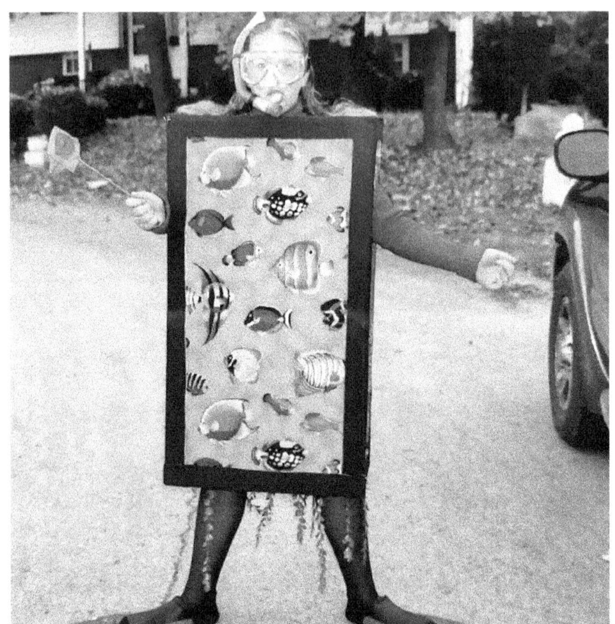

Winning Halloween costume, 5th grade

With Marley

On a bridge next to our pond on Brower Road

Before the prom, with Marty

Senior picture

Bringing Max home for the first time

On the patio of our villa in Arizona

Paradise in Scottsdale!

In the Sonoran Desert waiting for sunset

Family walk in the woods on Brower Road

At Brendan's college graduation

Brody, weighing only 7 pounds the day he came home

With Brody, on his first boat ride—Sacandaga Lake

Brody seeing his doghouse for the first time

A selfie taken on her couch, now featured on Kelsey's bookmark

At the marsh trail with Brody

Brody resting on the college campus after visiting with students

Photo of Brody later shown in the hospital newsletter

Now on Kelsey's headstone

Debbie's favorite picture of Kelsey

Acknowledgments

My heartfelt thanks to:

—Marty Waffle, my husband, for 42 years of friendship, love, and support, most recently as I worked on this project. He knew I wanted to share Kelsey's story to help others who are grieving, and he aided and encouraged me every step of the way.

—Brendan Waffle, my son, for always being willing to spend time with his mom, even as a teenager. Whether out to a movie, visiting Adirondack Animal Land, starting a new fish tank, or just going for a walk with our dogs, he was and still is a remarkably easy and wonderful friend and companion.

—Patricia Sweet, my oldest and most faithful friend, for countless afternoons of listening to me talk about Kelsey, helping me process what happened, and just letting me be sad—yet still finding ways to make me laugh and smile.

—Cathi Hanauer, my editor, who was willing to accept me as a client even knowing I had no previous writing experience, and who asked all the right questions to make this story complete. And to Cathi's mom, Bette Hanauer, who volunteered to be the first reader and offered many kind words of encouragement.

—Dr. Kenneth Chapman, the pain management doctor I visited in Manhattan after Kelsey died, for showing my daughter kindness and compassion and for treating her like a person who mattered.

—Marilyn Willett Heavilin for writing *Roses in December: Comfort for the Grieving Heart.* Her strength after surviving the loss of three children at three different times in her life was miraculous. Her courage gave me courage.

—Melody Beattie for writing *The Grief Club: The Secret to Getting Through All Kinds of Change.* So many people shared their stories with Melody so she could share them with the world. These people helped me feel normal at a time when I felt lost.

—Cider, Cocoa, Hershey, and Max, the dogs who will always be members of our family.

—Marley, the yellow lab who Kelsey saved, for being her roommate and best friend, and who now shares her resting place.

—Brody, for making Kelsey feel needed when it mattered most and for giving me the strength to imagine a future worth living.

About the Author

Deborah Waffle taught second and fourth grade for 33 years and is now retired. She and Marty have been together for over 40 years. They currently reside in Broadalbin, New York. Deborah and Brody visit several different medical facilities once or twice a week as a therapy dog team. Brody brings smiles to all the people and patients he meets. Deborah can be reached at Dwaffle16@gmail.com